Dr. Jaideep Singh Chadha was born on 11th of October 1949 in Mumbai. Having graduated from the Indira Gandhi Medical College, Shimla in 1972, he did his Post Graduation in Internal Medicine from the Post Graduate Institute of Medical Sciences, Chandigarh in 1978. He has authored two other books **Vinculum** and **The Funny side of Golf.**

He lives in Chandigarh with his wife, Gurminder. He was recently awarded the 'Vijay Rattan' award.

I think today the world is upside down, and is suffering so much because there is so very little love in the home, and in family life we have no time for our Children. We have no time for ourselves. Parents have very little time for each other, there is no time to enjoy each other and in the home begins the disruption of peace in the World.

—Mother Teresa

PLEASE, MOM! IT'S MY LIFE

Dr. Jaideep Singh Chadha

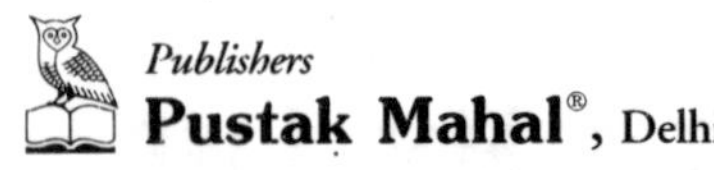

J-3/16 , Daryaganj, New Delhi-110002
☎ 23276539, 23272783, 23272784 • *Fax:* 011-23260518
E-mail: info@pustakmahal.com • *Website:* www.pustakmahal.com

London Office
51, Severn Crescents, Slough, Berkshire, SL 38 UU, England
E-mail: pustakmahaluk@pustakmahal.com

Sales Centre
10-B, Netaji Subhash Marg, Daryaganj, New Delhi-110002
☎ 23268292, 23268293, 23279900 • *Fax:* 011-23280567
E-mail: rapidexdelhi@indiatimes.com

Branch Offices
Bangalore: ☎ 22234025
E-mail: pmblr@sancharnet.in • pustak@sancharnet.in
Mumbai: ☎ 22010941
E-mail: rapidex@bom5.vsnl.net.in
Patna: ☎ 3294193 • *Telefax:* 0612-2302719
E-mail: rapidexptn@rediffmail.com
Hyderabad: *Telefax:* 040-24737290
E-mail: pustakmahalhyd@yahoo.co.in

ISBN 978-81-223-0937-9

6th Edition : April 2008

Printed at : Param Offsetters, Okhla, New Delhi-110020

Dedicated to

my mother
Ms. Herbhajan Kaur Chadha
who tried to teach me
but did not succeed.
My wife, Guggi, who is
my best friend and an angel.
To my children, Aman Deep &
Guneet, without whom life
would have very little meaning.
To Shiv Raj and Kabir, who bring
sunshine into our lives.

Contents

PART-III

PART-IV

Preface to the Fourth Revised Edition

One never knows what life has in store for us. I could never have imagined a fourth edition, let alone a revised fourth edition. But the response to PLEASE MOM! IT'S MY LIFE has been so overwhelming from all over the country that one is humbled. The beautiful mails that I have received from children and adults are most touching. Most of them started with "thank you for writing Please Mom…!!!!". As a mere mortal, expectation of some appreciation was natural, but the "thank you " part shook me till my teeth rattled.

Some young readers accused me of touching every aspect of life excepting their problem. I informed them that this book is far from complete. It is an ongoing process. It could become an interactive book and their problems would be discussed in subsequent editions (some of which I am discussing in this edition.) I took it upon myself to summarize the book. It turned out to be a tough proposition, if I may say so myself.

I was thrilled when Captain Sanjay Anand, Principal of Doon Public School, Punchkula, Haryana, informed me that he had included the book as a part of the compulsory curriculum for their senior classes. It is indeed an honour. There are feelers from other schools as well.

I was informed by another teacher that she noticed a new phenomenon in her school. She noticed children sitting under trees, on benches in the grounds and at places where they were normally not seen during recess. On enquiry, they were found to be reading PLEASE MOM, IT'S MY LIFE! Now, that definitely is a compliment, if there ever was one.

As I went through the book again, before I embarked on writing this Preface, I realized that my tone has changed as I progress to more complicated subjects. Not that these subjects concern senior age groups, it was as if I felt that the reader is maturing as he flips through the pages. At least I did.

I am happy to report that since the launch of the book at the INDIRA GANDHI MEDICAL COLLEGE ALUMNI MEET, on the 22nd of May 2006, held in Shimla, I have spoken to about 10,000 school children in Chandigarh, Punchkula, Kasauli, Kharar and Delhi. These sessions have been hugely uplifting for me. I hope I have helped the children too.

Introduction

In golf, they say any fool can putt it in the second time. And so it happened, that hindsight became notorious for the number of gurus it created. Gurus who have committed so many blunders that it is no longer funny. I have committed so many blunders in my life that they are ready to sprout, out of my ears! I sometimes dub myself a 'blunder pro', you know—as in golf pro. My mother should have warned me about things, since they say 'Mother knows best'. But Mother knows best about only a few things in the world of today. Even if she did know everything about everything, it would still have been futile, for kids don't want advice from mom. They think they know everything. That is where the blunders begin. At least mine did.

The other side of the coin is that if we don't learn from the blunders of others, then learning from your own would take a life time. Such learning proves to be no fun at all. And I don't want you to spend a lifetime learning from the blunders you committed and the fact that you could easily have gone through the slips or ducked. So I decided to write this book for you. It is basically for the younger lot, so that life can be a bit easier for them.

(I am sure it still will not be blunder-free passage because you will have your unique situations and sometimes you will have to look for answers yourselves. But then that is what life is all about. Learning!)

In my lectures at various forums and to different age groups, I stress my points with the help of anecdotes and short stories which aptly illustrate what I have to say. I would like to inform you here, **that these stories are not mine.** The authors might be dead and gone, but these wonderful stories need not be buried in the sands of time and disappear into oblivion. And if these stories help even a few of my readers, then the purpose is achieved.

There are many books written for children, which is a good thing. But books for adolescents and young adults are far and between. This is the category of our society which needs help, for this age group is neither here nor there. Parents, schools and society may have succeeded in confusing your young minds. Often you may end up taking the wrong step or taking help of the wrong stuff like drugs.

The present trend in the mind set of youth is that parents are not their well wishers. Parents are fine till they 'give in, all the time', but the moment they don't, they become public enemy *numero uno*. I would like to tell my young friends, that parents and not Anne or Rahul are your best friends.

What one sees today is that children are stressed to levels which are beyond the comprehension of the adult mind, especially parents, who want their children to be the best in every field and are shattered if they don't perform accordingly. They can't seem to comprehend the reasons for their child not topping, **all the time**. This stresses the children to no end, because they have to come up to their own expectations as well as their parents' and the school's. Somewhere along the line, society has also begun to demand its pound of flesh.

It is a matter of prestige for the school to have the best results in the region. It enhances the school's reputation as a centre which imparts the best education. Since that has already been accepted as the yard stick, nothing can be done there. Another yardstick which measures the level of happiness and contentment in students should be incorporated.

In your quest for success, you have forgotten the basic principle of life. Come on, people! Get real. We are not here just to study, get a good job and earn lots of money. Life is much more than that. Life has to be lived. We have forgotten to do that. God did not create schools, curriculums, jobs and all that... .....Man did. God did not make us divine just to work on a job. He wanted us to perform greater deeds.

And how is life to be lived? That is the million dollar question. I have attempted to help you get an answer to that one. Obviously, you have to search for answers which are suitable for you. What I have given you here is the first step to the ladder of life. To try and live a life that has the least stress. Ways to hit the ball through the slips or duck when life throws a bouncer at you. You will have to find and climb the rest of the steps or rungs yourself.

(author)

E-mail: jaichadha2001@yahoo.co.in

Acknowledgements:

- Special thanks to: Kimi Dhanoa for helping me.
- Bharpoor Singh & Manpreet Singh
  (Students of Govt. College of Arts, Chandigarh)
  for the lovely cartoons that they created.

Part-I

The Sculptor

I am sure some of you must have heard this one before. This story tells us a lot about ourselves. Even if you have heard it before, dig it out of the deep recesses of your brain, ponder over it and see how it fits in with your lives. This story is the summary of what I am going to tell you in this book. We will discuss the aspects of gratitude, the values of acceptance, surrender, our "wants", jealousies, instant gratification, patience, humour etc..

There was once a poor sculptor. He could barely make both ends meet. One night, as he was passing in front of

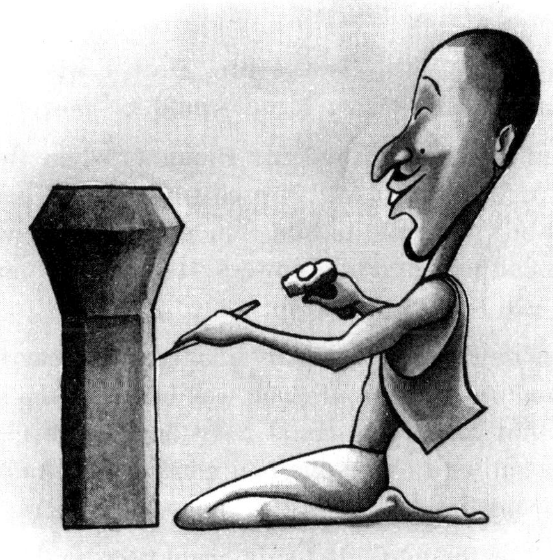

a rich man's house, he saw the owner of the house, relaxing with a drink in his hand and two servants attending on him. He thought to himself, "Oh, what fun it would be if I had a house like that and servants to do my bidding!"

Immediately, there was lightning and a clap of thunder and the poor man found himself in the rich man's house basking in the glory of his wealth. He began living the life of a rich man and was generally very happy.

Then one day, all his servants abandoned him and ran outside. He was very surprised and wanted to see who was more powerful than him. Outside, he saw a crowd gathered around a palanquin. He went up and saw a government servant sitting pompously in it, accepting the '*salaams*' everyone was giving him.

He said, "Yes, this is the life. How I wish I was a government servant. Then I too would be powerful...."

He had hardly finished his thought, when the same thunder struck and he found himself sitting in the palanquin with every one deferring to him. The once sculptor was now happy. He had never-ending powers. He could get any work done and get anyone in prison.

Till one day, he was again abandoned by his carriers and left high and dry. On enquiry, he was told that the sun was so strong that the people could not stand in the glare and heat of the sun and every one had gone to the shade of the tree for protection.

"Wow," he thought. "If I only could become the sun ..." And sure enough, he was the sun.

He made lives of people miserable, till one day he realized that no one seemed to be bothered by him anymore.

Perturbed, he asked, "Now, who is more powerful than me?"

The clouds, they said. They block your heat and rays. So it was no longer a terror for anyone. The ex sculptor decided that he has to be a cloud. When he became a cloud, he was happy. He produced rain whenever he wanted. He made the weather damp and dreary when people wanted sunshine. But one day, he lost control over himself and he was told that it is the wind that has taken over. He realized that the wind was more powerful. The cloud had no say in it. So he asked to be the wind hoping that he had at last found ultimate power. He uprooted trees, homes, whipped up storms and made life miserable for every one, till one day, he could not go where he wanted to go. Perplexed he asked around and was told that the majestic mountain was blocking his path.

He was infinitely impressed by the mountain. He thought this was the ultimate in power. So he wanted to become the mountain. When he became a mountain, he was very happy.

There he was, totally majestic! Till one night, he heard a sound "Kut,kut, kut....." On investigation he was told that a sculptor was cutting into him. And that was the time, when it dawned upon him that as a sculptor, he had been the most powerful all along.

Chew on it guys! See what you can make out of this one.

To Begin with...

There could be many ways to read this small book. You could read it slowly, chapter by chapter while you analyze it. Or you could read through quickly and then mull over it. In any case, the stories that I have chosen for you are not ordinary stories. They are like teachers. Learn from them.

The people of Punjab, the land of five rivers, are known for their zest for life. Their attitude is different. The way they talk, the way they walk, the way they eat and make merry is different. And now, thanks to MTV, you might have noticed, the way they sing is also different. So what is it that makes them different?

Punjabis were not always sure that they would be alive the next day, since Punjab was always in the thick of wars and attacked by enemies. Hence, they lived for the day, day by day. They just wanted to be happy while it lasted.

Today, despite the fact that there is so much poverty, malnutrition and addiction in the villages of the state, the basic traits are maintained.

But as you come down to the towns and cities, the difference between the Punjabis and the rest of the country is almost non-existent. Happiness is no longer seen. Sadness is camouflaged by addictions to drugs and alcohol. So basically, every one thinks he is happy, after sun down in case of alcohol and through out the day if it is drugs. Because, with that stuff inside them they don't know any better.

Unhappiness is the buzz word of this century. This is despite the fact that people have never had it so good materialistically, You will see a lot of people with a lot of money, but are they happy? Young children are unhappy in their homes, schools and generally. The ones who are in colleges are unhappy because they are so worried and tense about their future. The ones in jobs are unhappy because they want to go up the ladder and reach the top as of yesterday. No one wants to wait for the incubation period to be over. The unmarried ones are unhappy because they want to get married. The married ones are unhappy because they would rather be single. The ones who have children are unhappy because their children are not happy and they don't measure up to their expectations. The ones who don't have children are unhappy because they want to have children and they can't.

Yet, if I ask you, what is that one most important thing that we crave for in our lives, I am sure most of you will say ‘happiness’.

We go looking for it all over.....in materialistic things, supplements like drugs and alcohol etc. forgetting that happiness is already within us. If you peep into the lives of people from the state of U.P. you will find that quite a lot of them have migrated to other states. Invariably, they then make a monopoly out of trades like gardeners, vegetable and fruit sellers and rickshaw plyers. They have little money, almost no belongings, but they make us green with envy when they sing with gay abandon and enjoy life as if they have no care in the world. Chew on it and try to find out what makes them tick, when we, who have everything at our disposal, are looking for that thing called happiness and the lack of which gives us so much stress!!

The Experiment

I have gone through a whole lot of definitions of stress and I feel that this one is the best of them all.

STRESS IS THE DEMAND MADE UPON THE ADAPTIVE CAPACITIES OF OUR MIND AND BODY.

In the olden days, life was very simple, as you can imagine. The only mode of transport was walking till they discovered that animals could be tamed. The daily chores were limited. There were no wives and no husbands. Everyone belonged to everyone and no one belonged to any one. They did not have to make houses. They lived in ready made ones, the caves. The only competition was from bears and other animals already living in them.

The only stress they had was from carnivorous animals, which included dinosaurs. The stress lasted till they were under attack and then it was all over. Agreed, some of them must have died, but for the ones who survived, it was over very quickly. Then, as man got organized into races and countries and the institution of marriage was brought in, stress became a little more serious, but it was manageable. They even had wars, but the wars were short lasting though very intense.

The body had begun to get used to that kind of stress. You would know about the **'fight and flight reflex'**. When some one is attacked very suddenly, the body has a reflex which acts at the spinal cord level. The information about the attack doesn't even go to the brain. The spinal cord decides if the person has to fight back or run away. In either case, there are changes which take place in a split second. Some of the changes that take place are:

- The heart rate goes up, so that more blood is pumped into the muscles.
- The blood pressure goes up, roughly for the same purpose.
- The blood circulation to the skin and the stomach reduce, so that there is more blood available for the muscles.
- The gastric juices are reduced so that there is no chance of vomiting.
- The thyroid gland, which is the band master of the body gets activated and releases certain hormones, cholesterol (for energy) and sugar.
- The liver releases glycogen and cholesterol so there is more energy available.

Many more changes take place, all for the sole purpose of gearing up for the fight or flight. You will be surprised to know that these changes take place in an instant, without the brain coming to know. Now, when the dinosaur or the attacker has gone, the body immediately retracts the changes that took place, and there is no harmful residual effects in the body.

But, these days, stress is all levels. The home, office and every other place. Stress is omnipresent and the changes of the fight and flight reflex stay on and on, for days, weeks, months and years.Hence the following changes will become permanent:

- The pulse will always be high.
- The blood pressure will always be elevated, producing Hypertension.

- The blood sugar will be high causing Diabetes mellitis.
- The cholesterol levels will be high causing dyslipidaemia.
- The skin will be cold and dry producing skin diseases.
- The stomach will be prone to acidity and peptic ulcers.
- Oxygen free radicals will be released producing heart diseases, asthama. arthritis and cancer, to name a few.
- The brain will always be tense.
- All these changes will cause heart attacks and brain strokes.

The result is that stress produces a very sick man. Hence young boys and girls suffer heart attacks and wonder why!

There is a catch here. Not every one will suffer the bad effects of stress equally. Some will suffer more and some will suffer less because the end result will depend upon the person's reaction to the particular stressor.

It depends upon how well we adapt. For example, there is a group of boys who, in the middle of the afternoon ring your bell and run away and you are not able to fathom who or why anyone is doing that. There could be one person who is successful in nabbing the culprit, gives him a warning and lets him go. There could be another person, who nabs the kid, gives him a sound thrashing and then drags him over to his father. Now the father sees his son howling and is equally angry. Things could get very ugly here. Take a guess. Who has more stress. The person who had let the child go off with a warning or the second one?

At the other end of the spectrum, the reaction could come differently in different people if they were told that at precisely

5p.m., a nuclear attack from a hostile neighbouring country would destroy the city of Chandigarh. The person who thinks that he would rather do his favourite thing than sit around crying bucketful of tears, would definitely have lesser amount of stress.

So it is understood that it is our reaction to a situation that determines if we will have stress or not.

Stress is not a bad thing at all. If I tell you that henceforth, you shall be getting everything in bed and you are not to move a muscle for your wants, it will be great fun for a few days, but later you will turn into a vegetable.

The following experiment gives great insight to the value of adversity. An enclosure was created where special trees were planted. They noticed that after growing to a particular

height, the trees just toppled over. The organisers realised that they had failed to put in the wind factor. The lack of wind prevented the trees from swaying. This inhibited the trees from growing deeper roots. Thus, when the trees reached a particular height, they just toppled over because of their own weight, for the trees had failed to grow roots deep enough to support the tree.

Thus we know that man will also be like those trees in the experiment, if there was no adversity or stress.

I repeat here :

WHATEVER THE LEVEL OF STRESS, IT IS OUR REACTION TO IT THAT WILL DETERMINE THE OUTCOME. SO NO MATTER WHAT YOU ARE OR WHAT YOU DO, OR WHAT SITUATION YOU ARE IN, YOU HAVE TO ALTER YOUR REACTION IF YOU HAVE TO AVOID HARMFUL EFFECTS OF STRESS.

Be Positive

It is up to us to keep ourselves in the best mood. There will be so many things happening at school or at home or at the play ground that are bound to put you down.

Make sure that you control your negative emotions and see how you can make them positive. We will look into that as we go along.

I read a lovely little piece the other day.

There was once a farmer who trained his dog to walk over water. To show off his dog's unique ability, he invited his friend for a shoot. He shot a bird which fell into the river. He then commanded his dog to fetch it. The dog happily ran over the surface of the water and brought back the bird.

The farmer looked at his friend and waited for a comment. When there was none, he asked his friend if he noticed something different in his dog.

The farmer's friend said, "Yes, I notice your dog can't swim!!!"

This is exactly what we do. Some of us see the hole and some see the doughnut, some see the glass as half full and some half empty. Our lives will change according to how we see the world.

Influencing Factors

Factors which produce stress are:

- Personal
- Interpersonal
- Familial
- Social
- Financial
- Environmental

Unless there is a unique reason, the factors can be only these. One great reason for stress is when there is bereavement in the family and one doesn't know how to tackle it. This sort of a thing would come under the personal category. The inter personal one is when we have a misunderstanding with someone in the family, or at school and then as we grow up, in the work place. The environmental factors are the ones at the work place which produce some sort of conflict in your minds and you get all stressed up. The working hours could be prolonged, the lunch break could be too short for your liking, the boss might be too tough, rude or maybe just the vibes are bad.

In school, or the university, things might not be what you thought they would be. Or the studies are too tough or the subject that you chose out of peer pressure is just not your cup of tea. All these are reasons which we have to identify and then get on with life. **These days the pressure generated by parents is well known to cause enough stress on the child to take many a wrong step**.

Children are very intelligent these days and they are fully aware of the problems they face to fight life. If society and parents don't help and they become the stressors instead, then it becomes all the more difficult for the children of today.

The omnipresent financial factor is too well known. And the stress this puts on people is serious enough to make them commit suicide. You know of the poor farmers of AP and Punjab who committed suicide, by the dozens.

And then it is not just the poor who are in financial trouble. The ones who are apparently rich might not be rich in the real sense of the word. The problems they might have would be of a greater magnitude. They too give up and commit suicide. It is something like in battle conditions. One man turns into a hero and the other into a coward who flees the battle field and gets a bullet in the back.

The social reasons could be equally important. Just imagine two people of different castes fall in love and they are hounded by both communities. Can you imagine the amount of stress generated for these poor people. But then many a brave ones have fought it out and prevailed. Like I said, it is how you react to a given situation that will determine the end product.

Descarte said "I Think Therefore I Am"

It is said "We are what we think". That is what moulds us. Most of us are, unfortunately negative thinkers. For us, the glass is always half empty. But we have to convert our negativity into positivity and that takes some doing.

The great philosopher of yesteryears Descarte said :

I THINK THEREFORE I AM

This 5 word sentence was considered the summary of life for years and years. It basically meant that I can think therefore I am superior to animals, I can think more than you, therefore I am superior to you and, finally, I can think more than every one else, so I am superior to everyone.

Modern day thinkers like ECKHART TOLLE, then realized that all of mankind's stress problems arose just because we think all the time. In his book, "THE POWER OF NOW" he tells us about the voice which berates us all the time and then we retaliate by putting forth our own arguments. Since that voice is our conscience, we can't beat it. The result is a kind of a tape that keeps running in our head. The remedy is to imagine the most comfortable sofa and place it in a corner of our brain, sit in it and when the voice starts up, be a silent listener, and don't answer back. The whole thing will stay as a monologue and a monologue can not sustain itself. It will die its own death. This state of mind is called the "GAP OF NO MIND". It is similar to the state we reach during meditation.

It looks easy, right? **Wrong**! It is a difficult thing to achieve, but then nothing comes easy in life. One has to practice this one. As is often said, "PRACTICE MAKES PERFECT".

90-95 % of our diseases are self created, because of stress. Even accidents are caused by our stress or by the other man's stressed mind. One could be so engrossed in problems, that the mind is not on the road while driving, thus causing accidents. People could take wrong decisions while they are at important positions and could cause great harm to many people.

Because of the same stress, levels of cholesterol, sugar and hormones could change, producing disease. The blood pressure goes up causing hypertension which could later cause heart and brain diseases.

Thus, you can see that it is important to stay happy and stress free and one has to learn this right in the beginning and not when it has already caused us great harm.

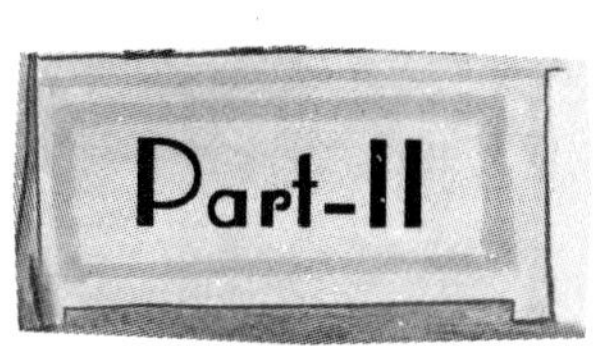
Part-II

Attitude of Gratitude

WILLIAM JAMES, THE FATHER OF MODERN PSYCHOLOGY FELT THAT THE GREATEST DISCOVERY OF OUR TIMES IS THAT WE CAN ALTER OUR LIVES BY ALTERING OUR ATTITUDES!

So now we will go on to learn various methods to control our stress.

As they say, first things first. There has to be a change in our attitude to life and how we perceive it.

You might think that I intend to sermonize you to death. No! I intend to sermonize you to a happier and a fulfilling life. Obviously, this book is not for people who are not receptive and the first attitude is:

Attitude of Gratitude

Sometimes we wonder, "What did I do to deserve this?" or "Why did God have to do this to me?" Here is a wonderful explanation!

A daughter is telling her mother how everything is going wrong, she's failing algebra, her boyfriend broke up with her and her best friend is moving away.

Meanwhile, her mother is baking a cake and asks her daughter if she would like a snack, and the daughter says, "Absolutely mom, I love your cake."

"Here, have some cooking oil," her mother offers.

"Yuck," says her daughter.

"How about a couple of raw eggs?"

"Gross, Mom."

"Would you like some flour then? Or maybe baking soda?"

"Mom, those are all yucky!"

To which the mother replies, "Yes, all those things seem bad all by themselves. But when they are put together in the right way, they make a wonderfully delicious cake!"

God works the same way. Many times we wonder, as to why He would let us go through such bad and difficult times. But God knows that when He puts these things all in order, they always work for good! We just have to trust Him and, eventually, everything will be wonderful!

God is crazy about you. He sends you flowers every spring and a sunrise every morning.

Whenever you want to talk, He'll listen. He can live anywhere in the universe, and He chose your heart.

We have taken ourselves and this life and the world we live in for granted.

So, my first request to you would be to stop doing that. No one in this world owes us anything. On the contrary, we owe many things to many people.

We owe our existence TO GOD.

BUT

The first thing that we must do is to acknowledge the existence OF GOD.

So, every morning, be grateful to HIM. Thank him like you have thanked never before. Go down on your knees and thank GOD for everything that he has given you. This life, a healthy body, parents, friends your country. And then don't forget this for the whole day. At the end of the day, thank him again for taking you through the day and his blessings.

Then thank your parents for bringing you into this world, for giving you a lovely home, good things to eat and wear, good education and the finer things of life.

Then thank your country for giving you what ever it gives you. Thank your brothers and sisters for the love they give to you and society, for making you a part of it.

Once you have shown your gratitude to all and sundry, you have achieved a very rare state of mind. i.e. **HUMILITY.** You have realized that the world owes you nothing. On the contrary, you owe your existence to so many factors.

Realization is the first step to success in what we are out to achieve collectively.

In school, and years later, I had the notion that teachers were my enemies...that they were out to torture me.....because in those days, my mind was mostly on sports and comic books. So home work and I were fairly distanced. I would "forget" my homework copies and assignments. The excuse "I forgot" was so rampantly used by me, that my friends in class thought that my middle name was "I forgot".

My favourite nun in school was Sister Liliana. For some vague reason, she too had a great fondness for me and would often *complain to my* mother that *I was her favourite*, but she had no idea why I wasn't interested in studies. And mind you, I was more interested in playing cricket and badminton than in studies.

The footrulers, in those days, were made for strength and not for beauty as they are made today. *Sister Liliana had*

***mastered that impliment to perfection*, not to draw straight lines, but to make the likes of me realize that I was in school not to play, but study. Moreover, in her hands it became a musical instrument, and it made wonderful music which went kut-kut-kut on my knuckles and thuk-thuk-thuk on my palms.**

Between the footruler and sister Liliana, I was made to realize that sports and studies went hand in hand......and one could not do away with either of them ....I mean teachers like Sister Liliana and the footruler. And I am proud to say that these two made a man out of me, finally. Somewhere down the line, if one has a good and loving teacher, that teacher alone would be responsible for a lot of geniuses in this world.

Of that I am sure. Even after 45 years, I salute Sister Liliana, where ever she is.

Attitude of Surrender – To the Almighty God

In life, we have seen that as we become more and more confident of our abilities, we tend to try and solve all our problems by ourselves. But then there are some problems in life that are beyond us. Unknowingly, in our ignorance we keep trying and trying, banging our heads against the wall, so to say. Nothing happens and we get very stressed out. We forget that there is a higher power than us out there, who is our great friend. I agree, it is our duty to solve our own problems, but if we fail because of some reason, then instead of getting stressed, just turn to GOD and say, "GOD, I have tried real hard and failed. This is your problem now and you solve it for me."

Once you have handed it over to God by acknowledging your helplessness, that you have surrendered to him, you will immediately see that it no longer bothers you as much as it did before. Because it is no longer yours. It is GOD's. But first try yourself – Real Hard. Otherwise God is going to get heavily overburdened.

See. NO STRESS!!

Attitude of Acceptance

The next most important attitude to destress ourselves is the Attitude of Acceptance.

There will be moments in life which will be very difficult to explain away. The question WHY ME? will loom very large on the horizon. No one can give you the answers to that question. Then the stress is automatic. Should we let ourselves be stressed? No, definitely not! Under those circumstances, if you learn to accept it and repose your faith in GOD, you will not be stressed. You know about Sant Kabir ji. He was a great visionary of his times. Even then, he had realized the importance of the fundamentals of stress. You know, in his times when there were no taps and no running water, the most important thing in a house wife's life was a 'matka' or a pitcher to store water, to be used for the kitchen and drinking. Now if that broke, the house wife should ideally be shattered. But she says:

> *Attitude of acceptance*
> *Bhala hua meri matki phuti rey*
> *Main to paniya bharan sey chuti rey*

"It is good that my pitcher has broken. At least I have been spared the ordeal of having to go miles to fill it up with water. That, my young friends, is total positive thinking for you.

So Who Said Life is Fair?

How many times do we hear this "WHY ME, GOD! WHY ME?" if we are afflicted with some physical abnormality or a disease or we take a dip in life because of losses or anything which we don't like happens, we instantly cry out "Why Me?"

ARTHUR ASHE, the only black American ever to win Wimbledon said:

"Why is that when we win, we never say "WHY ME, GOD?" It is only when we lose we say "why me"?

As a fall out, one must realize that we should accept the good with the bad.

Another aspect of acceptance is accepting authority. Just like the boss has authority over the rest of the staff, it should be accepted that parents have authority over children, the husband has authority over the wife, the mother-in-law has authority over the daughter-in-law. If the rightful authority is denied, then there is conflict. And conflict breeds tension and the entire atmosphere is vitiated.

The rule to be followed here is :

the acceptance of authority

There is no shame or loss of face in accepting authority. On the contrary, it only shows your upbringing and your virtue of humility.

After all, you too would not keep a servant if he or she refuses your authority and keeps answering back or refuses to do the chores you have asked him to perform.

The reason why there are so many problems in families in respect to children, in-laws, newly married couples and siblings is the **lack of respect for each other** and **the denial of authority**.

Attitude of Happiness

There are three things closest to the gospel truth.

FIRST, that it is our duty and our right to be happy.

SECOND, that happiness is not something that you get off the shelf in the supermarket. It is in us.

THIRD, that you have to work on your happiness, so that it grows. Be aware of it, Expect to be happy. The universe will listen to you.

I came across a wonderful story.

A cat watched the spectacle of a small kitten trying to catch its tail. After a while it got irritated, and asked the kitten, "And what are you doing?"

The kitten replied, "In the kitten psychology school that I attended, "we were told that our happiness lay in our tails. So, I will be totally happy when I catch my tail!"

The older cat replied, "In our times there were no psychology schools. We grew up in alleys. But we were aware that our happiness was indeed in our tails. But instead of trying to catch them we just went towards our goal, our destiny, and our tails followed us. And so did our happiness!!"

KAHLIL GIBRAN, the famous Lebanese philosopher (1883-1931) said that happiness and sadness are the sides of the same coin. The *Ying and Yang* thing. **He said that the "cup of your happiness is deepened by your sorrows!"** A person who has never encountered unhappiness in his life can never understand the full gravity of being happy, because he hasn't lived life to the fullest. In a life lived fully, there has to be some share of unhappiness too. As the sun rises after night, as the light comes on after darkness, so will happiness follow unhappiness.

In his writing "THE CREATER", he writes that God created a spirit from Himself and gave her the cup of happiness and said, **"Drink not from this cup unless you forget the past and the future, for happiness is nothing but the present."**

Eleanor Roosavelt said, "No one can make you happy or sad without your permission!" When we are happy, we laugh and laughter is the shortest distance between two people. You can laugh or you can cry, the choice is yours.

You can laugh at the most serious of problems. Only then, you can say : "I CHOSE to laugh."

There is a famous saying, "When you laugh, the world laughs with you, but when you cry, you cry alone"

There is another aspect one learns from the fruit kingdom.

If I ask you to squeeze a ripe lemon very tightly, what will come out of it?

And if you answer, "Juice, what else", you will be absolutely right. Because what is in the lemon will come out. Don't expect diamonds to come pouring out. So if life or examinations or a stress full situation squeezes you, what will come out?

Simple! Whatever you have inside of you! If you have happiness, happiness will come out. If you have anger, hatred and unhappiness filled in you, what will come out of you? Exactly those very things!

Now the lesson that we learn here is

- that happiness is our birth right,
- we don't have to go and catch it; all we have to do is to make ourselves aware of the happiness inside us and
- to get rid of negative emotions like anger, hatred and unhappiness!

One More....

There was once a prostitute who used to live next to a temple. The priest in charge of the temple was very curious as to what the life of a prostitute was. He would peep at her when ever he got a chance to get away from his duties. Then he would wonder what she does with her customers and frankly, his imagination would run a riot. He developed a bad picture of her mentally. In fact she became an obsession with him.

The prostitute, on the other hand, would get up in the morning, take a bath, do her prayers and then look at the temple and at the priest, oblivious of what the priest was thinking about her. She would imagine the priest to be so lucky that he had a chance to be with God all the time, and that he had such pure thoughts. How she wished she could do what the priest did. After some time, both died. God sent

the prostitute to heaven and the priest to hell. The prostitute was dumbstruck.

"Lord. I have always been involved in a dirty trade and you bring me to Heaven, whereas the priest was always near you and you send him to hell? Why Lord?"

And God said, "What you did was your profession, but you always had pure thoughts. Where as the priest was meant to have pure thoughts, but he always had impure ones. That is why you were brought here and the priest was sent to hell."

This story further substantiates the fact that you are what you put in and what comes out also depends on what you put inside yourself.

Attitude of Forgiveness

The next important thing which we must learn is to have : **An Attitude of Forgiveness**

All of us tend to get very angry with the **person who has harmed** us. **The wrong could be real or imaginary**. We tend to harbour that anger within us. We even have the feeling of guilt for some act that we have done in the past, something which we don't actually approve of. We keep beating ourselves with the whip of such guilts. When we harbour anger against others or ourselves, we become our own worst enemies, causing stress to be built up. **We have to learn to forgive**.

There is a great story about two Tibetian monks who belonged to a sect which does not allow them to have any interaction with women.

> *Attitude of Forgiveness*
> *Jesus said, "Before you enter the temple, forgive"*

Once, both of them were on a journey and they came to a swollen river. They noticed a young woman standing on the bank, too scared to wade into the water. Without speaking, one of them hoisted the girl on his shoulder, waded across the river to the other side, and dropped her off. He then carried on with his journey. The second monk caught up with him, but didn't talk to him, for two hours and was seething in anger.

Finally, he blurted, "You know we are not even allowed to talk to a woman and you had the audacity to carry her on your shoulder. You should be ashamed of yourself."

The first monk said, "See, I have already taken that woman off my shoulders two hours ago, whereas you are still carrying her on your shoulder!"

Wonderful!!

If only the second monk had understood and forgiven the first monk, he would have not been so angry and stressed out for those two hours and maybe more!

There is another dimension to this forgiveness thing.

When we don't forgive ourselves for the deed we might have committed, a need arises to punish ourselves repeatedly. And that need leads to a very poor image of ourselves.

I too had a list, a mile long in my mind. I maintained a sort of a black book there and in that I had kept records of what my mother did and what my brothers did to me ever since I could remember. I was very bitter. Anyone would be. Not only that, I had kept a record of all the acts that I did of which I was uneasy about. After all, everyone does something or the other of which he is not entirely proud. But since I never let myself forget, I was succeeding in creating a very poor self image. When I read this story of the two monks, I tore up my mental black diary, forgave all those who had been unfair to me and then I proceeded to forgive my acts which made me uncomfortable.

Believe me, when I tell you that since then I am a much happier person.

Forgiving doesn't mean that you forgive a person who has harmed you by going and embracing him, knowing fully well that he is going to stab you in the back. Forgiving him means, that you mentally forgive his action which has harmed you and at the same time, realizing that this person is not reliable and that you need not have any ties with him. It would be foolish to forgive such a person and make up with him only to be harmed again. Forgive him mentally and harbour no grudge against him. Then, forget that he ever existed. There should be no thoughts of vendetta.

Attitude of Perfection

One aspect of our psyche is the feeling that everything should be perfect. We should be perfect, our parents should be perfect, our siblings and friends and our world should be perfect.

Purn madhay purn midham
puranth purn mudhachatey
purnasya purn maadhaayey
purnmevavashishyatey

This Sanskrit shlok when translated would mean:

This is perfect that is perfect. When we take the perfect from the perfect, what remains is the perfect.

There is a gem of a story which illustrates this perfection aspect very well.

Once there was a swamiji, who was on a journey with his disciples. As darkness approached he called for rest and announced that he will bake chappatis (pancakes) that night. The disciples were thrilled for they had never seen their guru baking chappatis. Wood was cut, a fire started, dough was kneaded and the swamiji was ready to bake chappatis on the *tawa*. The first one was a complete failure with the chappati being burnt. When he tried to take it off the tawa, it broke into a hundred pieces. But the swami was totally satisfied with his effort and said, "Perfect". This surprised the brood of disciples. Then the second attempt chappati turned out triangular with holes and the edges were burnt. When he scraped it off the tawa, he again uttered "Perfect" The disciples were even more surprised. The third one turned out to be square and that too broke into many pieces. He had to

literally shovel the pieces off the tawa, and he again said "Perfect." By this time, one of them was ready to pull his hair out. He blurted, "Swamiji, why are you making a fool out of us? Not even one chappati is round, yet you call them all perfect."

Swamiji smiled and said, "I was waiting for you to ask me this question. You see, you could not have eaten the dry flour, you would have choked on it. You couldn't have eaten the wet dough. It would have got stuck in your throats. To prevent you all from going to sleep hungry, I had to bake it. That is what I have done. Who said that for a chappati to be perfect, it has to be round? Perfection is only your perception of things."

In God's world, everything is perfect. **It is only our perception of how things should be that makes it imperfect**. And that is where our anger at imperfections begin. Order wise, we have land, water, oxygen, nitrogen, carbon monoxide, food in plenty, but then we need transport, designer shoes, clothes and watches, refrigerators, cars and air conditioners, different foods in restaurants. And if our mothers provide us with almost everything and only one is missing, we blow our tops. We are hopping mad. We call them all sort of things and stress them and ourselves.

The question is, why can't we accept our world the way it is?

Why must we change it? We should change ourselves for the better instead and our world will change with us.

To begin with, most couples pine for children. When children are born, the same couples start comparing them with other peoples' children. And in a split second, they find a host of aspects which they wish they could change. Did God promise every parent a beauty queen or Buddha? A wife like Saraswati or a husband like Yudhisthir or Ram? A man or a woman marries accepting everything about the partner. But the very next day, he finds that the wife snores, applies mascara, doesn't know how to cook well. So does the wife discover a hundred things about her husband which she would like to change as of yesterday!

Why can't we accept things as they are? Actually we should. If you don't keep your expectations too high, your stress levels will be fine.

Attitude of Non-criticism

Let's talk about the **Attitude of Non-criticism**

We have nominated ourselves critics of this world for we criticize all and sundry. We don't even pardon ourselves. In fact we are our worst critics. We tend to pulverize our self esteem so badly, that there is no need for others to do that. Who needs enemies?

Even if the lad in question is a strapping six footer with enviable looks, the usual dialogues go something like this, "Me? Are you are talking about Me? Look at me ...What am I? I am just a naval officer (mind you, he earns 3000 US $ a month at age 25). Who will marry me?

"Look at my face. Does this look like it launched a thousand ships? Well this face can't even launch a paper boat. Man, I am UGLY, as in U-G-L-Y!"

Hearing this, are you sweating or what? I sure am. My friend's son was a handsome Sikh boy. One day, he got his hair chopped off. The reason? "Girls in my class don't want turbaned boy-friends!!!"

So after getting his hair chopped, did he become the local Casanova? Take a guess? With self depreciating attitude like this, he is lucky that he is going out with himself, let alone hopes of winning the Nobel Prize!!!!

If you play golf, and you happen to hit a good drive and your playing partners applaud you, all you must say is thank you! Not "Wait till you see my next shot. I will go into the out-of-bounds or shank it or most likely duff it." "Me? I can't stitch 4 good shots even my life depends upon it." That is exactly what a lot of people do. And what happened to their game? You guessed it! Right first time.

Normally, poor self esteems are the handiwork of dissatisfied parents, who couldn't achieve their life's dream and now want to achieve them through their children or because of over critical teachers, or when we compare our worst with the other person's best. If one is a carpenter, he shouldn't put himself down by comparing himself to a doctor. Agreed that he can't do a doctor's job, but can the doctor do the carpenter's job? Or a good student pushes himself down because he can't play cricket like a pro. But can the cricketer produce grades like yours?

If we have to love our parents, siblings, neighbours or the whole world, first we have to love ourselves, for charity begins at home.

Similarly, we should **respect ourselves** first and then we respect others.

We have to **forgive ourselves** and then we learn to forgive others. We have to see the beauty in ourselves and then we see the beauty in others.

We have to **accept ourselves** first, for what we are and what we are not, and only then will we accept others.

If we call ourselves ugly, and call others beautiful, it is bound to produce feelings of acrimony and self depreciation in ourselves.

See, every one in this world has good and bad aspects. It is like ying and yang, two sides of a coin. A pessimist will look for the bad stuff. What I would like you to do is to look for the right stuff. But also do remember that without the wrong stuff, there is no way for you to see the right stuff. After all, if there were no bad people, how would you know who are the good ones? Be comfortable with your negative traits. Know them well and just keep an eye on them lest they go out of hand. Just don't flog yourself on their account.

The other aspect of criticism is the **acceptance** of criticism. One should accept the criticism from others as healthy criticism and listen to them and then analyse it yourself. Healthy criticism is good and the critic should not be taken as one who dislikes you.

But, if the person takes it upon himself to criticize you on everything, then I suppose he should be ignored or asked to keep his opinions to himself.

So,
LOVE,
RESPECT,
FORGIVE AND
ACCEPT

Yourself, before you accept others.

Attitude of Approval Seeking

Another aspect which is bound to cause great stress is the **Attitude of approval seeking**

If we go back to the time a child is born, every new thing that he does, every new word that he utters, the first step that he takes, the first spoon of food that he puts into his mouth, everything is applauded and a pat awarded for his deed. Even when he goes to school and then to college, he keeps getting those pampering pats of approval. He gets into the habit of receiving them and when he goes for his job, he begins to expect a pat for everything that he does. And when he doesn't get the pat that he is expecting, he goes into a tizzy. He just can't comprehend the fact of life that sometimes you are doing your own thing. You are getting promoted to a higher class when you pass, you are getting paid for the work that you do. So, why can't he do the job and get on with it. Those who can, are not stressed and those who can't understand this basic thing, will create problems for themselves and others. It is like a doctor who is meant to save lives, goes into depression if he is not applauded for saving a life.

It happened to me. Once when I was on duty, a man was brought in with a cardiac arrest and I happened to revive him with methods taught to us. But instead of feeling happy about it, I felt miserable for days. I hit upon the reason after a week of wondering. I had not been applauded by the patient, his relatives or the senior staff of the establishment for whom I was working. I had to explain it to myself that it is my job to save lives. I have been trained to do that and if I have succeeded, why should there be any patting? I felt much better after that realisation.

The trick my dear friends, is to delete this ingrained aspect of our psyche. Go for NON APPROVAL and say no to this attitude of approval seeking.

And while we are at the topic of saying NO, I must tell you another important aspect of our lives. Most of the time, when we are asked to do something, we will say YES irrespective of the fact that our brain is screaming NO. But just to be NICE, we say yes. Now starts the conflict between the heart and the brain. The brain has said NO, but the heart has said YES. This conflict will lead to immense strain.

If you don't want to do something for someone or you don't want to give your favourite thing away just because your friend has asked you for it, then say NO very emphatically. It is better to say NO, once, than to be upset for the whole time.

Divide Your Life into Compartments

One sure way to curb your stress is by dividing your life into compartments. Divide your daily life into 4 compartments.

- Home
- Work
- Personal
- Social

A bit of intermingling will always be there, but as a general rule they should be sealed compartments. One thing which is definitely required is that there should be no mixing between home and work. For the younger ones who are still in school, their attempt should be to plan their lives for the future. Obviously, they

can't keep their school activities from home. But for them the four compartments can't exist for they are not working. For them school is their workplace and studying well is their job. Socializing is not an important part of their lives. It is just a means to interact and relax when they are not studying. It is said, "All work and no play, makes Jack a dull boy."

There is a story that I simply must tell you here.

There was once a farmer whose farm house was very old. He called in a plumber to fix a tap. But when the plumber tried to open the nuts, he found they were all rusted. His wrench broke and then the rusted pipes broke. With great difficulty, he finished the job. By then he was a very tired man. He went to his truck and found that one of the tyres was flat. That was the last straw. He became very angry. He asked the farmer to drop him home. As they were driving, the farmer noticed how angry and sullen the plumber was.

When they reached the plumber's home, the plumber invited the farmer into his house and the farmer accepted.

Before the plumber rang the bell, he went up to the tree outside the house, held a branch between his hands, bowed his head and lo! He was a changed man. He rang the bell, was greeted by his dog, children and then his wife, each of whom he hugged happily. He laughed a lot, drank and ate a lot and then it was time for the farmer to leave.

Before he sat in his car, the farmer said, "You were so angry before you did something to the tree. What was it that you did there?"

"Sir, I have one principle in life. I never take my work problems home. You know what a tough day it was for me. If I had taken my anger inside my house, everyone would have suffered. So, I go to the tree every night and tie my

bundle of problems that I had during the day. I then request GOD to look after them for the night and that I will collect them in the morning. But the next morning, the problems in my bundle are very few. Tomorrow, my tiredness will be gone, my truck will be repaired, my wrench will be replaced. So why should I bother my family?" replied the plumber.

Wow! Isn't that great?

The next compartment which should simply be segregated from the rest is your personal compartment. This one is totally yours. You can read, listen to music, play your favourite game or go to the gymnasium or you can simply do nothing! No one, and I mean NO ONE should be allowed to interfere.

Then, do not let your personal life mix with your social life. Every one in this world has problems. So don't go and start telling other people about yours. No one is interested, believe me. They have enough on their hands already. It would be very rude on your part and stressful for the others if they are very polite and have to listen to your ravings. If you are upset and in a very bad mood, do not go to the party, if offloading is your aim. But if your aim is to have a change of scene, where you will meet interesting people and you hope to forget your problem, then definitely go.

But no OFFLOADING, please!

Time Management

FOR EVERY SIN, BUT THE KILLING OF TIME, THERE IS FORGIVENESS

—A SUFI SAYING

A very closely connected aspect of life here, is **Time Management**

If we manage our time well, then there is very little scope of getting into trouble at school or at work for arriving late, not being able to complete your assignments on time, etc...

Have you noticed the speed at which people drive their wards to school in the morning, the frayed tempers, how they jump traffic lights and the subsequent accidents that occur? This

happens every morning, because either the child hasn't been trained to get up on time and get ready on time or the parents are late in starting from home.

Shrieks of, "Papa, we will be late. The gates are going to be locked!" splinter the early morning calm. This suddenly converts papa into a Grand Prix race driver and all hell breaks loose. There is another thing that has been taking place all through. The child is being conditioned.......

- that, it is alright to jump red lights
- that it is alright to speed up
- and then, it is alright to abuse people.

This very thing is sure to be incorporated in the child's mind and the pattern will be repeated.

People often ask me how can I do so much: that I write, that I practice medicine in the clinic and then make house visits at all times, day or night, that I play golf (which takes time), that I party, go to the club, socialize etc. I tell them that God gave me 36 hours in my day. Actually, friends, I suppose it is good time management. Being a Sikh, one has to keep time allotted to the fact that we do take longer to get dressed, than those who have short hair and who do not have to tie a turban. I have never felt short of time, because I know all that I have to do is to get a head start (literally)!

You do that and see how it changes things for you. You will be prepared for your exams ahead of your time, you will never be late if you keep some time in your kitty for those small traffic jams, the red lights, the occasional flat tyres, the unexpected phone call as you are leaving, etc.

And you will never be the LAST MINUTE MAN. And you will never be stressed.

Instant Gratification

> *Infants and Instant Gratification Mode*
> *vis-a-vis*
> *God's universe*

A phenomenon unique to the animal kingdom is that the new born comes to know the moment it is born (and once it has its bearing right, which is very quick) that the mother is duty bound to feed it. But it is only in the humans that the child also realizes that if it makes a ruckus, the mother is going to feed it in extra quick time. Having realized that, the child grows up demanding things and if it doesn't get what it wants, it will remember that crying and shouting always is a winner.

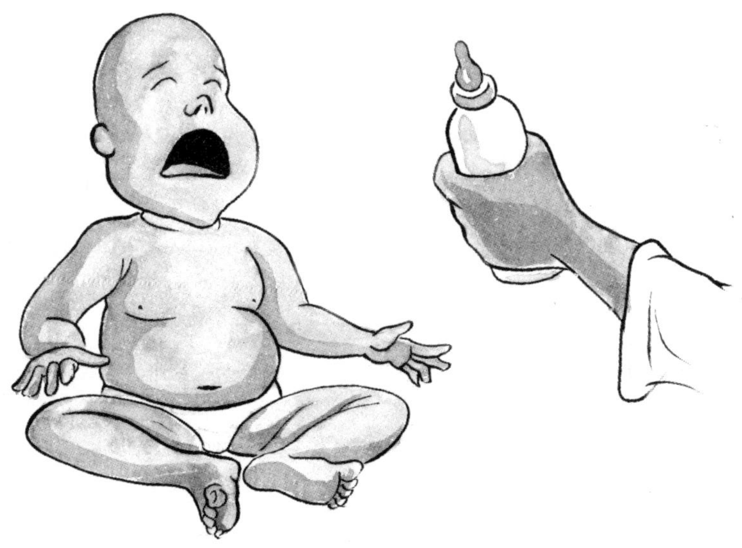

This is called INSTANT GRATIFICATION.

When this grown up child goes to school and then to college and to work, it carries on doing the same things, only now it is larger tantrums in the form of strikes. And he succeeds everytime.

Then he tries doing it with God...... I want this and I want that. But you see, in GOD's world, everything is preordained. No amount of crying will help. You can't go on strike against God's establishment. It is best that we understand that what we need here is patience. What God has to give us will be given but in HIS sweet time and not when you want it. So unlearn the phenomenon of instant gratification and learn the art of PATIENCE. There is no need to hit your head against the wall. Often we stress ourselves and others by this behaviour.

The Great Blame Game

This is one aspect of our lives that we go ballistic about. Nothing in this life ever happens due to our own fault, or our own doing. If we have a poor self image, it was our parents who maltreated us when we were small, or our teachers did it to us. If we don't have what we want, we blame God and every one we can think of. For once, **we have to learn to take responsibility for our -selves and our actions.** If someone turns to drugs, it was because his parents did not understand him when he was a kid, there was too much violence in the household. Or his parents did not care for him. Another fellow takes to crime, he says his parents never provided him with enough, so he had to look after his own needs. If he turns out to be a bad egg, then society was responsible for not throwing up good enough role models.

We must realize that for once, we have to stand up and be counted.

Take responsibility for your self.

If your job is to study, do that and do it well. Nothing must come between you and studies. If you work for some company, then your company work should be a priority. When you went to work for that company, you joined it knowing all the pros and cons, the pay structure and the work load. So don't play the blame game there, saying that the boss is bad, the co-workers are jealous, or the work environment is not conducive, etc…Loyalty to the company should be on the top of the priority list. You have no right to go on strike. Work for the pay that you get. If you do not like the conditions, just leave.

If you are married, do you remember that you got married after you accepted your spouse on your own free will, accepting the good with the bad. Don't start the blame game and destroy your marriage. On the contrary, accept your partner for what he or she is and make it work. If after you have tried everything and it doesn't work you should make a clean break from the marriage without any mud slinging. This is one golden rule to avoid stress, Have you come across couples who have divorced, but still say, "We are the best of friends." And you must have come across warring couples who divorced, but call each other names and are enemies for life. Which one of the two do you think have more stress? There are no special marks for this one though.

A Story in the Middle

Two of my favourite members of the animal kingdom are the donkey and the duck. The donkey first. Have you ever seen a more misunderstood and more abused creation of God? Frankly, I haven't. But the donkey bears it all with a poker face and

sometimes even with a grin. Once in a while, when it is really fed up, it does give a kick to whoever may be unlucky to be standing behind it. Another thing, have you ever seen donkeys fight or get involved in a gang war like others do? Even birds have wars. The reason is that the donkey is totally egoless which is mistaken for lack of the grey matter in the upper storey. It doesn't keep defined territories. It will never assert the right over an area as dogs do. It has accepted its role of a burden manager and goes forth doing it for the food, shelter and the looking after that it gets. That is a total picture of a stress free zone.

Now the noble duck. We get an adverse shower of luck and our world crumbles around our ankles. Learn from the duck. Even if there is a cloud burst on it, it doesn't let a drop of water linger on its feathers. It doesn't show off like man when it is working. It paddles away softly below the water and goes on towards its destiny.

Learn from these two animals and keep stress away.

The Now

Have you noticed that most of us either live in our past or in our future. It is very rare that a human being lives in his present. We are either worried about what happened in the past and its ramifications, and carry the guilt around our necks. Or we keep worrying what will happen twenty years from now or even tomorrow. Even your parents are so worried about what you will become twenty years later, that they forget to enjoy what you are today. They will be after you to go for tuitions at age 3, they will worry that you were fourth in the class instead of coming first. There was a news item recently about this young mother, who killed herself because her daughter had not done well in the 10th class. As if the 10th class or her future was more important than the mother's life. Now that she has departed, who is going to see what her daughter has finally become?

Then there are those students, who commit suicide in the most horrendous manner if they even suspect that they have not done well in their exams. So what, man? So what if you haven't done well this year? There is always next year or the year after that. You tell me... does it really matter?

There are two days in our life which we can safely forget. One is the day which we call yesterday and the other one is tomorrow. We can't change yesterday's events because these events have already "happened." Similarly, tomorrow hasn't come yet and what hasn't happened, cannot be altered because we don't know what is going to happen. So, why worry about these two days?

Here is a wonderful quote :

**"YOU CAN'T CHANGE THE PAST
BUT,YOU CAN RUIN A PERFECTLY GOOD PRESENT
BY WORRYING ABOUT THE FUTURE."**

That is the whole problem with all of us. None of us live in our present, something which we should be doing.

OK, let me ask you if you have a problem as of now, now! I mean this second. Most of you would be either lying down and reading this book, waiting for your servant or mother to announce dinner or lunch, or you must have already finished it. You have a roof over your heads ; you have a school, college or a job to go to; most of you have had a good education or are going through the motions of acquiring one, your parents have a good or excellent financial position, so you would be possessing most of the stuff one need to entertain oneselves. So at this moment, you lack nothing.

But are you the happiest of them all? Maybe not. Because you would be worrying about something that has happened or some thing that is going to happen, **according to you**.

My advice to you would be, stay in that moment and move to the next when it comes and so on. ...Moment by single moment!

Stress in students has increased tremendously and this is reflected by the number of suicides being committed by them. Psychiatrists call it a mass hysterical chain reaction. It is a very disturbing trend. My advice to students is to take their studies in a happy sort of way. Studies can be fun too.

As far as results are concerned, one tends to agree that the population of India is so huge that sheer numbers increase the competition and students are bound to get stressed. To them, I say, imagine the "WORST CASE SCENARIO". What can or what will happen, if the result is not as expected? You will lose one year? Or may be two? Or you will not get into the professional course that you or your parents so badly wanted you to do.

So what? One year out of a person's life is just 365 days! It is definitely not the end of the world. Maybe that profession wasn't your cup of tea. You were meant to do something else. Destiny has other plans for you. Do not underestimate destiny.

Think about it. Would this matter one year from now? Or, will it matter 100 years from now? The answer would most likely be "NO".

But if you commit suicide because you can't face disappointment, what is going to happen? This life is a gift from God. You are too important for your family and to your country. You will lose it, never to get it back again.

SO, NEVER COMMIT SUICIDE. DON'T EVEN THINK ABOUT IT.

There are some youngsters who kill themselves because their boy friends or girl friends have jilted them. So what? Any one who doesn't realize your true worth is not worth dying for anyway.

If society doesn't let you get together, fight society. You should have the courage of your convictions. If you desire the person so much, then you have to be ready to fight for him or her.

Giving your life is just another way of saying that you are a coward. That you gave up. That you did not have it in you. There could be an agitated one who could say "Yes. I can't fight it. I am a coward."

To him I would say that a living coward is better than a dead one "Laugh at life, man. Don't take it so seriously. In fact don't take anything too seriously. No one is permanent here. Enjoy while you can. When the time to go comes, depart, happily."

On 16th of May 06, a little girl committed suicide, thinking her marks would not be good enough. When the result was declared, unfortunately after her death, she had scored 96% marks and topper! What good did her death do for any one? It was a precious life lost in vain!

On the 4th of June 06, a girl had the guts to face an oncoming train, she committed suicide for not doing well in her BA exams.

If only she had used her courage to fight lifes battles for one more year!

But what actually happens in life is a bit different. No one really wants to die **(excepting the suiciders)**. In a study of terminal cases of cancer and who wanted euthenesia, it was found that none of them wanted to die in the pain free periods of their illness. Even in their pain, when asked if they were ready to accept death, each one of them refused!

JUST REMEMBER—LIFE IS PRECIOUS. TREAT IT THAT WAY!

Jealousy

JEALOUSY, surprisingly is the single largest reason for heart attacks and stress! Surprised? And I would be not very far from the truth, if I said that this was the single largest reason for stress since time immemorial. If you go back to the story of man's origin

in the HOLY BIBLE, jealousy was the reason why Kane killed Able. The reasons could be any and could be quite mundane.

But sibling jealousy is number one on the list. Siblings get along well usually, till they are married, then acrimony between the siblings will begin because of wives, children, different financial status and the materialistic holdings and finally over property matters.

Next is the jealousy in school, college, work etc.

My advise to you would be to stay far from jealousy. It is like cancer. It eats you up from inside and then you can't do anything about it. Even our pets have the same trait. If you pet one, the other is ready to eat the one being petted.

The donkey wins hands down in this situation, for there is no jealousy here. You can drive in your Mercedes car or live in a palace, pet as many donkeys you want, it will never be bothered. Learn from the donkey. What is yours is yours, what you have to get, you will get, for GOD will see to it. But by feeling jealous you will get nothing, only your blood pressure will rise and your brain will start working overtime to plot ways and means to bring the other person down and to make him suffer for no fault of his.

This is exactly what we don't realize... that we are what we are and everyone is dealt a different hand by God. There is no need to be jealous of others or their achievements. If you can emulate their achievements in a happy sort of a way, good. Otherwise ignore the issue. For each to his own.

If you crumple a crisp 100 rupee note under your shoe or grind it into the mud, the monetary value will be the same. Similarly, if at any point of our lives, we are also down or crushed, we too will remain basically the same. Our value will remain the same, all set to bounce back. So there is no need to loose one's self esteem over a temporary situation. Jealousy does that to us as it reduces our self esteem.

Often we are in a hurry, as of yesterday, that we be promoted or that we become rich. If we don't, then we get very upset and try to take out our anger on those who have been promoted or are rich. We forget that those who have succeeded, have put in their share of time and effort. We will also get our due ….in due time.

Sometimes, we are so jealous of the people ahead of us, that all logic seems to abandon us and we sincerely feel that we are more deserving, more intelligent and hard working than the one who is our senior. There are chances that you could be right …..but by being jealous there is no way that you could get what might be rightfully yours. Like I said, all at the right time.

There are other methods by which we can lose our self esteem. Sometimes, we are helped in that direction by our parents, siblings, class mates, teachers and society. These are real reasons why some of us put ourselves down.

But sometimes, we put ourselves down by letting **one failure in one project mean that we are failures for life. Or, comparing our worst with someone else's best**.

For example, a plumber compares himself to a doctor saying that the doctor knows so much about the human body, knows how to treat so many illnesses. He begins to get an inferiority complex because he can't do all that, forgetting all the while that the doctor can't do what the plumber can do. So, remember the golden rule, one should not compare two non comparables.

The Attitude of Receiving and Giving

Giving and receiving are the two sides of the same coin. If there are no receivers, there can be no givers. One should be a graceful receiver, be it blessings, knowledge, money, gifts or any material that the giver might want to give to you. By refusing. you embarrass the giver. Accept the gift with grace and gratitude. I remember, I presented a gift of nominal value to a multi millionaire friend of mine. This friend was also my senior in age. But the grace with which he accepted my gift made me so happy. That happiness was more than any happiness I would have felt, had I been on the receiving end. It wasn't that he could not have bought it himself. Accepting does not make you inferior to the giver because you never asked for it in the first place. On the other hand, if God has put you in a comfortable situation where you have more than you will ever require, then you should be magnanimous and give. By giving, you not only help the needy but you also keep what is God's, in circulation. Money has been called currency, or current.It is productive if it remains in circulation. By storing it in banks, it ceases to be in circulation and like blood, clots. I am not rich by any standards, but when the need arises to give, I give and wonder of wonders, it comes back many folds.TRY IT! Have you noticed your friends blowing up thousands of rupees in a restaurant, eating pizzas and other so called exotic foods. Next time suggest to them to eat at home and donate the money they would have spent, to a needy family. See what happens. That family's eyes will light up. They will bless you with all their heart and that money will keep them happy for days, if not months.

TRY IT! Another thing will happen. That pizza that you did not eat will have such a good effect on your health in the coming years. And if you make this a habit, your life is made. India is full of philanthropists, but of a different kind. They give, but only to further their own cause. One hears of people giving anonymous offerings at Thirupati temple in crores of rupees. In Hyderabad, there is a huge statue of Lord Mahavira and they bathe it once in 12 years. They have an auction for the privilege of being the first person to pour milk on the statue. The auction this year went for a mind blowing 1 crore and 36 lakh rupees!!! This got me thinking. This gentleman spent that much money for a religious belief. For his own benefit. Mankind had no role in the larger scheme of things for him. If he had only spent that money on a 1000 families, wouldn't they have blessed him collectively? Similarly the crores of rupees that people offer to religious institutions, which incidently have enough money of their own, does not have any philanthropic benefits. On the other hand,we know of an unending list of philanthropists in the West, who will give large donations for a cause. It might be for earthquake victims in an unheard of place in India or Tsunami victims in a remote corner of the world. They might give for research into a rare disease. But they give for a cause. **Do you know how many people in India do NOT give for disasters in India?** How do you expect them to give for victims of Hurricane Katrina in New Orleans? My point here is that we must give, give and give. I agree that the designer shoe and the wrist watch is important. But giving is equally important.

Attitude of Self Righteousness

There was once a holy man who was meditating under a tree. Suddenly a young man who seemed extremely distressed, ran up to him and said that people were after him for a robbery that he did not commit. If they catch him, they will cut off his hands. So he was going to hide in the tree. He also pleaded with the holy man not to tell his pursuers.

Shortly, an equally agitated group of people arrived and asked him if he had seen a boy go past. The holy man pointed upwards into the branches and the boy was caught and his hands were chopped off.

When the holy man died, he was asked by GOD, as to why he did not protect the boy. The holy man said, "I was a holy man and lying was not in my character. I would have lost my self respect had I lied."

God said, "No! You were wrong. Just for your self righteousness, you sacrificed the young man who had come to you for help. What good did you do him or to yourself?"

Many a times, we come across situations where we are asked to help out some one just because it is in our power to help. But at that point, we put ourselves on a pedestal bringing forth the fountain of our own righteousness. We deny that help to a person, who desperately needs it at that point of time and not our beliefs. It could be a teacher helping a student, a doctor helping a student who has missed some classes and will miss a whole year, if the doctor doesn't give him the certificate of illness. A person could lose his job and so on. So keep your priorities right and decide.

Sometimes, we know something about some one which could hurt the man immensely...... should it become public. We now think we have great power over that human being. You tell me, what should be done in this situation? After all, you have the information!

Attitude of Adaptability

In life we are faced by many painful situations, where we could get emotionally hurt. The best way to sort out these is not by reacting against them, but by adapting yourself to the situation. Here I will give you the example of the shark.

> *Adaptability*
> *The Shark*
> *This Remarble Creature Adapts To Its Surroundings So Well That, In A Small Equarium, It Will Stay 6 Inches, But When Shifted To The Ocean, It Will Grow To A Length Of 6 Feet*

The shark as you know is a very deadly fish, but it is also a great teacher for the willing student. If you put a small baby shark into an aquarium, it adapts itself to the size of the aquarium. It would grow to roughly 6 inches. But then, if you transfer the same shark into the sea, it will grow to the customary 6 feet! The pun here is that a fully grown shark will not shrivel down to 6 inches! Just to adapt, that is.

We should adapt ourselves to our situations and the environment instead of fighting it and creating great stress for everyone, especially ourselves.

Most of the times our ego doesn't let us function as we should. And what is ego? In the words of Deepak Chopra, it is the mask that we wear all the time, of who we are socially. We could be anybody in real life, a doctor, a CEO of a company or a lawyer. This role playing becomes a must, because our ego generates fear of loosing the post which we so assiduously protect. It is always, what if….. This attitude prevents us from adapting to so many situations in life and thus the stress. Your father could be a Judge or an I.A.S. officer on a high and important post or he could be a big politician because of which you could be also suffering from an ego problem and could easily become a bully. The behaviour pattern is the same as in the adults.

What we learn from here, is that there should be no ego related to the position held by your parents. If this happens, you would automatically be more humble and would not create problems for anyone. Have you noticed that quite a lot of the brawls and crimes committed are by the children of the categories I have mentioned? Their ego goads them to do things they would not have done, if their parents were not who they are. Again the fear is that they would lose all the privileges, if on a later date, their parents are no longer on those posts.

Am I making some sense to you here? This is a complicated subject, definitely. Only a few of us understand this aspect. Later on, as we progress in life, we will not take up a job saying this is beneath me and this does not behoove my stature. I have very little ego and if there is a job I can benefit from, I will do it, irrespective of the fact that I am a doctor. I know of a lot of doctors who want to do the same work, but their egos will prevent them from doing it.

This brings us to the most pressing problem that our youth face today. How to juggle a career and marriage!

Since everyone is convinced that marriage is something that everyone has to go through, so they marry, but without being prepared for it.

The youth of today believe that they need to be earning huge 5 figure salaries and only then can they make both ends meet. The term "make both ends meet" has taken up a very different meaning these days.

What they have to understand is that money is not the only thing which keeps people married. There are a lot of adjustments that the couple have to make, otherwise their marriage is in for a rude shock as so many couples are finding out the hard way.

The key here is adjustment. There can not be two equally placed people in any partnership for one has to be in charge. In olden times, the lady of the house was apparently subjugated, but the way I look at it, she was the mistress of the house in the true sense. She used to decide every little matter pertaining to the house and the children, though on the face of it, it looked like the man was running the show. Matters are a little different these days with the husband and wife expecting to be on equal footage.

There is a grave shortage of respect for each other. Age or sex is no longer the automatic granter of superiority in any given relationship. So how can any one expect the relationship to last. There is bound to be conflict over each and every issue. The end result doesn't have to be imagined. Moreover, our young couples give more preference to their careers than children.

Children are the reason why people marry and should marry for, and are the binding force in a marriage and if that force is also absent, the writing on the wall is in capital letters. The major question that has to be answered is:

Then, why marry at all?

Do you think you can answer this one?

Children get lawful recognition only if they are produced in a wedlock situation. Hence, if the natural human urge to be parents has to be fulfilled, in today's society, one should marry.

If there is no urge for parenthood, then the need for marriage is non existent and two people can stay together as they are doing these days all over the world.

In the West, people have gone ahead and produced children out of wed lock due to their overpowering urge for parenthood. Once there is a conflict between the two parents and since there are no legal bindings, they are free to go on their separate ways. Some children are abandoned and there are others who are luckier to be brought up by a single parent. Let me assure you that none of the parties involved is in a happy situation. There is great stress all over and this is of a long duration. The lifelong excuse for these children, if they become criminals, will be that they were neglected children.

The Moral of the Story is: If you believe in the institution of marriage, and if you think that you can shoulder the responsibility, then by all means, go ahead and get married. But also remember that one reason to get married is to procreate. If there is no desire for children, then why marry at all? But then, there are those who marry for the want of a companion who he or she loves. As Osho puts it, the moment two people marry, love goes out of the window, because then the issue is that of a legal binding where the law is brought in, for the protection of the parties. The trust has already gone out. The stress that is generated is whether one companion will be faithful or not. Will he leave me one day for some one else? If he does that, where does that leave me?

If there are no expectations in a relationship, there will be no stress.. For this, one has to have a big heart. If you have that, only then can you proceed in your chosen direction.

Bad Habits

Sister Aloysius told us in school that we add one strand everyday to the rope called HABIT till it is strong enough to pull us up or take us down, depending upon the habit being good or bad.

She also told us about the SEQUOIA TREE. The sequoia tree is one of the largest trees found in the world. There is story of one such Sequoia tree in the north of America,

somewhere in the Grand Canyon. It was hundreds of years old. It had weathered storms, lightning strikes and ferocious winds. Then a parasite decided to enter it and make it its home. It laid thousands and thousands of little parasites which ate up the interior of the sequoia tree. When the rains and the winds came, the sequoia tree, which had been standing for ages, toppled over.

Friends, our habits, if they are bad, are like the parasites which ate up the insides of the sequoia tree. We too fall like nine pins. But if we have the strength to cultivate good habits, we are the giant Sequoia tree.

Humans, my friends are attacked by many species of parasite like habits and they cause great harm to us. The biggest harm is what is fashionably termed as STRESS!

I am not saying that people should not smoke. After all, cigarettes are meant to be smoked. One decides to smoke only after a conscious decision and the end result has already been accepted by the smoker. If he has accepted to die a few years sooner or with an associated disease, so be it.

It is like going to see a movie which you know has a lot of vulgar scenes. The movie is there. The choice of seeing it or not, is your decision. If you take a conscious decision to see it, then you have lost the right to criticize it for its vulgarity.

Smoking should be a conscious decision by the smoker and not just a habit. If he smokes just out of habit, it will cause him greater harm. Osho has some things to say about smoking as a habit. He compares smoking to the Zen tea ceremony. There is a special place for it, a special style for making the tea, serving it and a special style for drinking it. Tea is had in great awareness, even the way it is sipped is special, he says.

Similarly if you want to smoke, don't smoke as if it is a sin. It should only be done in a special room, and in a very ritualistic manner. Talk to the cigarette, take it out slowly, tap it on the box and since light is a deity, why not a lighter, for it gives off light. Light it up and smoke it very slowly, being in awareness all the time and take your own sweet time. You will feel that slowly the body will not crave smoking, because it no longer is a habit, but a matter of choice. If you want to leave smoking, you will, very easily be able to give it up. Since you have decided to smoke only in a special room, the number of cigarettes that one smokes, is also less.

Personally, I feel that smoking is public and personal enemy number one. Not only does it destroy the person who smokes, but also the unsuspecting one sitting next to him and his family members. The smoke coming out as a side slip is a worse carcinogenic stuff than the one that goes into the smoker. So think about it. We do owe it to society, don't we?

Doctors and executives have a problem here. They are huge smokers for some reason.They tend to ignore the deluge of data and studies done on this subject. **BY THE WAY, ONE CIGARETTE IS SAID TO PRODUCE 3 TRILLION OXYGEN FREE RADICALS.**

My favorite philosopher, JOHN LOCKE SAID "**TRUTH IS NOT THE TRUTH. TRUTH IS ONLY WHAT YOU WANT TO BELIEVE!" If you believe that smoking causes greater harm to you and to your family, only then would you like to do something about it.**

Kudzu Vine

I would like to tell you a very interesting fact of history. In the 1930's, scientists in the U.S. realized that soil was rapidly eroding in the south of USA. Nothing seemed to help and then they hit upon the kudzu vine. This vine had the distinction of having roots which went very deep into the soil. They hoped that the roots would hold the soil together.

So the Kudzu vine was planted all over the region and they waited with baited breaths. No one knows what actually happened to the soil, but the kudzu vine literally took over that part of America. It went over fences, trees, electricity poles, wires and anything else which stood long enough in one place.

This book is not about the soil of America. I am here to tell you that we also do something which we should not be doing. We have imported the corporate culture, the pizza culture, the hamburger culture, the culture of pornography etc from other countries.

These have taken over our society in exactly the way the Kudzu vine did and are throttling our very existence. I call it the Kudzu Culture.

Along with the corporate culture came **stress** in a big way. Boys and girls don't want to marry, because they would rather have the corporate life. If they do marry they don't want to produce children. If they do agree to produce children, they stop at one. And then they come to the full circle because they can't look after the child and go to work at the same time. This produces stress in their married life and all kinds of problems arise.

If you seriously analyze the effects of the cable TV, what do we have? Easy accessibility to adult movies with their bad effects on children. The cartoons that they watch consist of scary looking characters who have no other work than to destroy each other. Even the benign looking cartoon show "Tom and Jerry" consists of only bashing each other up in all sorts of violent ways. The only difference is that the whole thing is camouflaged in such a way, that no one actually gets killed in the end and they survive despite third degree methods like blasting with dynamite, hitting each other with every conceivable article etc.

The food habits are so atrocious because of the junk food, that Indians are sitting on a time bomb of diabetes and heart disease. Hamburgers, pizzas, pepsi and coca cola have a great role to play and unfortunately this will plague many generations to follow.

Declining morals are but a natural fallout. It was once said, "What you can say, you can see and what you can see, you can do!" And it all started with the four letter word but now it is acceptable to all classes of society.

The stress that all these have produced on society and on the individual in our country cannot be imagined. How it can be undone will prove to be an insurmountable problem. I feel that each of us will have to tackle it at an individual level and maybe, one day, God willing, society will be purged.

Unfortunately, there is so much money involved in these things, be it smoking, fast food, pornography, alcohol or drugs that those who are involved in these trades will fight it all the way.

The realization and the will to change things will prove to be most important.

ALL YOU SHOULD DO IS:

- Stop drinking colas
- Do not eat pizzas & Hamburgers
- Stop smoking
- Do not take drugs.

Patience

There was once a great Sufi teacher, Sari, who was asked to talk about patience. As he went forth his explanation with great wisdom, he was stung on the foot by a scorpion, not once, but many times. The great teacher ignored the stings and carried on. The event had been noticed by his disciples, who asked him the reason for not moving his foot out of harm's way, the teacher said, "How could I? Here I was giving you a speech about patience, I could hardly give you council and advice on that subject without being patient myself. I would have been ashamed before God."

This is one trait which is in total short supply in this generation. Apart from the fact that some of us have impatience as an inbuilt trait in us.

Hence, we say that he or she is a very patient person. But most of us mortals have to develop this trait and it requires a lot of practice.

Have you noticed that most of us know one or two people in our class or place of work who irritate us to no end? I am sure you have some of this breed around you. There is no need of avoiding them. On the contrary, try to spend at least half an hour with them on a daily basis and try not to get irritated, no matter what they do, for this is a sure way to practice patience.

You must be wondering what is so important about patience. First let me ask a question. We see that people today don't even want to wait for their turn. Every one wants to break the queue. And if God forbid, they have to wait, they get so upset that their stress levels reach sky high and they explode. This applies to almost all activities … may it be driving on the road, in the bank when you want to conduct any transaction, if you want to meet an official or if you want to see a doctor. Every one is in such a tearing hurry that they would go over everyone's heads, literally.

So be cool, be patient and you might live longer.

The lack of patience in today's generation is fairly evident if one goes by the disputes between couples, with their in-laws, between siblings, socially and at the work place where the juniors have no patience for their seniors and the seniors have no patience for their juniors. Every one is in such a tearing hurry without knowing where they are going.

Anger

I might as well tell you that nothing that God created is without its uses. It all depends upon how we use HIS gifts. I must tell you an anecdote here.

Once upon a time there was a farmer.He had a son who was very short tempered. As a result, he would get into arguments and fights and as a result, spoilt relationships. The farmer decided to teach him a lesson. **He told his son that every time he gets angry, he should hammer a nail into a very beautiful table that the family owned.**

The first day, the son had to hammer 28 nails and after dinner, he told his father about it. The next day, he was more conscious about his anger and he had to hammer in only 20 nails. Finally, there came a day when he did not have to hammer a single nail. He went to his father beaming from ear to ear. His father was very happy. **He said "Son, now for every anger free day that you have, take out one nail."**

The son did that and soon, he had taken out all the nails. He went back to his father and told him that he had taken out all the nails. His father was again very happy and together they went to the beautiful table. The farmer made him stand three feet away from the table and asked him to examine it. He told the boy how disfigured the table looked with all the holes in it.

"It will never be the same again. When you say things in anger, they will be leave scars like these. No matter how sorry you feel later on, the hurt will linger. Things said in anger are as bad as causing physical wounds."

The farmer's son understood what his father wished to convey and for the rest of his life used his anger sparingly.

Anger has its good points too. I am not asking you to do what the farmer's son did. But in certain situations, anger goads you, pushes you into performing better, raising your bar to greater heights. But the golden rule in life is to keep it under wraps. Your family, friends and colleagues will like you better and you will also be a happier person.

Personality

I agree that God has made every one differently, thus there are the personality types and sub types. This is a subject in its own right. But having said this, let me add that the knowledge of your personality type should help you to change for the better. Let me give you an example.

Type A people are always fighting the clock for they want to succeed! These people will automatically be very short on patience and will call stress and its complications on to themselves. But they can't help it, despite the fact that they have been told about this.

Type B is the slower version of type A. They are comparatively laid back and accept that they will achieve their goals maybe today or sometime in the future.

Type C are the ones who couldn't care less. Maybe, they wait for God to give them their due. But there are many more character based sub types of personalities and it would be a good idea to go through a larger book on personality.

In a recently concluded inter school story writing contest, the comments by the judge were eye opening. She said that stories coming from these children were either very sad or full of anger. It was as if the children had lost their childhood in the rat race of education.

Dear, friends! I couldn't agree more with her. One rarely hears childish laughter, we don't see children playing for the sheer fun of playing a game. Competitiveness has crept into every aspect of our lives in such a way, that no one can enjoy anything any more. There will be some who say that they enjoy their game of golf or chess or whatever game they like to play. But watch them. If they are losing they don't enjoy the game all all. So who says they are playing for the fun of it. When one plays for the fun of playing, then a good or a bad shot isn't the end of the world and neither is

the end result. Hence, people have stress even when they are playing a benign game like cards. Competitiveness is good, but only to a limit.

What can one expect from a child when he comes to an empty home? The parents are away to work and the child is left to his own devices. And when they do come home, there is no hug, but queries of how he fared in school and how many marks he got in the test. If he fared badly, he gets his share of scolding and if he does well, there is only a small word of praise. But mostly, the enjoyment factor in their lives is missing.

Friends

There was once an eaglet which got separated from its mother and was brought up by a hen. As it grew up, it began behaving like a hen too. It just walked along with other hens. It had no idea that it was meant to soar into the heavens and fly, till one day, it saw some eagles sitting in the trees. Majestic creatures they were! It was fascinated by them. They flew off after a while and the little one looked at them gliding in the skies with a grace, the eaglet had never thought possible. It wanted to fly too. But it did not know how. After many a failed attempt, it finally flew off into the skies and joined other eagles, and did what they normally do.

Thus the saying that 'birds of a feather flock together'.

Birds can't help it. But you, as humans, can sprout feathers of your own choice and choose the kind of people you want to spend time with.

You should choose friends who are supportive, who are good human beings and who will help you take the right direction in life. It is no good gravitating towards people who will teach you wrong things and who will have a negative influence on your life.

Why is that many teenagers gladly destroy their lives by joining the wrong group? There are many reasons. The road on which the good and hard working ones travel is difficult, time consuming and could be termed, monotonous. The rewards are also slow in coming. Whereas, the wrong road seems very exciting, for depravity has no limit. Starting from petty violence, loot, robbery, drugs, smuggling, prostitution and finally murder, it has many possibilities. **At the end of the tunnel, they can also see quick money. What they can't see is the road which ends in a coffin.** For the ones who don't end up in prisons and mental asylums, die early and very violently. Of that I am certain.

There is a middle path which many children and adults have begun to tread. This is an extremely dangerous path. 'The path of drugs.'

All categories of society have an easy access to this. It starts very innocuously. It could begin with a single puff of a cigarette, a sip of alcohol or the first sniff of cocaine. All for fun. The first of everything is very enjoyable. It is a great experience I am told. But then, as they are all habit forming, the craving slowly takes over. Then the demand overtakes the supply. Since these banned substances are very expensive and are not a part of the pocket money, **the problem that now surfaces is: how to finance the habit?** To earn money and to support their addiction, girls are lured into prostitution, pornography and the trade of couriers. Boys gravitate to a life of crime and then sink deeper into the quagmire of depravity. After some time, they barely know if they are coming or going. As they grow up, some marry with the habit and destroy their marriages as well. Some can't bear it and commit suicide or die because of overdose. We have umpteen examples of such people.

So you can see, where these people go. Do you, for a moment, think that these people knew nothing of the ill effects of these substances? You are wrong. Everyone knows. They have been warned, like I am warning you. I am certain that some of you will call me a fool and end up addicts. Why is that? Because everyone thinks that he or she is different from others. They think they have the capability to stop whenever they want to. Are they right? NO! Nothing is further than the truth. No one, I repeat, no one has the capability to stop once they are addicted. They might want to, they might even end up in rehabilitation centres. But once they come out, majority of them will end up doing the same. This becomes a vicious cycle and ultimately, end up as we know they will end up.

I know some of you will cite examples of some of our better known personalities. But the story for them hasn't really ended. In any case, these are very few. I know a lot more people who have not come out of the habit even after spending huge amounts of money. These are the lucky ones who have caring parents; who have forgiven them and are still ready to spend money for the rehabilitation centres. But are all addicts so lucky?

REMEMBER: DRUGS ARE A NO..NO..NO!!!!! PLEASE. If you so desire, I'll go down on my knees.

The easiest way to destroy a country is to put its citizens on drugs. Exactly like we were when the Britishers took over. At that time, we were on all kinds of addictions on our own. The British did not have to work very hard. All our Maharajas were already what you call "postis". Look at the state of Punjab now—we were the hardest working lot. Now we are hardly working. The granary of India, we were called. And now? Most of the farmers are on drugs and alcohol. No addiction is enough for them. They are taking in everything, from Lomotil tablets, 70-80 a day to iodex on bread, that is if they can get bread. And our politicians feed them alcohol and opium during elections so that they don't even know whom they vote for!

Fear

The fear factor is all prevailing. The fear of failure, the fear of ridicule, the fear of loss, fear of death.....these are the fears that literally rule our lives at all stages of our existence, more so in the formative years of our lives. Our self image takes a knock out punch because of fear. Are you getting it now? This is the beginning of our egos. As I said earlier on, ego is the mask of our social status, of who we are in life and it is all fear based. So try to banish fear from your life. Look at fear, right into it's face.

Why worry about death for we started dying the day we were born. Stare at death and your fear of death will vanish.

Value of Silliness

Silliness is not silly as in silly. Silliness has a relevance of its own as a stress buster. Remember how you talked to the 6 month old infant, producing funny noises, uttering unintelligent words, wanting the child to understand whatever you said or did not say? Just go back and try to recollect the happiness it gave you. And just picture yourself while you were 'talking' to the child. Did you look silly? I bet you did! Did your talk sound silly? Definitely! But imagine the happiness it gave you. Similarly, see how people talk to their pets. Agreed, dogs are said to have a vocabulary of 80 odd words, but they have to listen to all the woes of their masters too.

It is alright to let your hair down once in a while and be as silly as you want. When people go to discos, you think they are dancing? No, they are not. They have no place to even move, but they keep hopping. Look at the faces they make while dancing. One would have thought that they are in great pain. That is another aspect of the silliness that I am talking about. Then, when it is all over, they go home and recall how much they enjoyed themselves!

We are forced to look, talk and behave intelligently all the time, even if we are not. This charade, when enacted too many times produces stress. Hence, if you want to behave like children some times or even like idiots, it is alright.

Since you don't become intelligent and matured just by acting intelligent and matured, similarly, you won't become a silly child or an idiot if you act silly or like a child occasionally.

Humour and Laughter

Sometimes I feel that my only strength is my humour. I am not terribly intelligent or good looking. I am not a saint and I am not a very ambitious man. I believe that I will get what God has to give me. So I don't find myself running around in circles. Some call me a failure ......maybe I am. But I am certain of one thing that I am a humorous man, even if I may say so myself. What is humour? Humour is not the ability to create laughter by making fun of others. It is the ability to make others laugh at your expense, being able to laugh at your bad situation and it is the ability to see the brighter side of life even if is dark.

Some call the ability to tell jokes and make people laugh humour. Yes, that is good too. It is a quality that a few people have but then such people can becomes terrible bores, because the moment they have two people around them, they start off with their jokes which they have already repeated a dozen times. They will make sure that there is no other conversation taking place. They will often pick up one friend or one person from a given profession and then proceed to embarrass the gentleman till the whole gathering gets peeved. Come on! If you think this is humour, then you have another one coming. The only sound that any one can hear, is his voice and the forced polite laughter from a thoroughly bored audience. Instead of being a stress buster, such humour becomes a stresser.

Humorous is also being a good listener with the ability to laugh at a funny man.

Humour to a large extent is inborn, but it can be cultivated, to be happy and to make other people happy. Humorous people are not court jesters all the time but there are times and occasions when they are serious as well. But where stress is concerned, the humorous person will belittle problems to an extent, that stress barely has any affect.

Unfortunately, since humorous people are happy people, they tend to take life less seriously and as a result they are often a little rotund. Remember Julius Caesar commenting, 'that he likes being surrounded by fat people and beware of people like Cassius, who have that "lean and hungry look', for such men, think too much and are dangerous. If Cassius was a little fatter, I would have been happier'.

By being humorous, one can defuse any tense situation. By and large humorous people de-stress any gathering they grace. In other words, keep people happy.

So try to laugh a lot, all the time. Laugh with the world. Laugh at your blunders and mistakes, big and small. But don't laugh at the predicaments of others.

HUMOUR HAS IMENSE VALUE IN MITIGATING STRESS. IT IS SAID,

- LAUGHTER IS THE SHORTEST DISTANCE BETWEEN TWO PEOPLE.
- YOU CAN LAUGH OR YOU CAN CRY,THE CHOICE IS YOURS.
- REMEMBER WORRY, ON THE OTHER HAND IS INTEREST ON TROUBLE BEFORE IT COMES.
- IT NEVER ROBS TOMORROW OF ITS SORROW, BUT SAPS TODAY OF ITS JOY.

WE CAN DEFLATE ANY CONFLAGARATION BY HUMOUR. BY JUST LAUGHING IT OFF.

Part-III

Physical and Mental Fitness

One very important aspect of stress busting is fitness of the mind and body.

All that I have spoken about till now is dealt with at the beta level of our brains. This is the level at which we use our intelligence, argumentative powers, mathematical ability etc.

When we do an EEG test, 4 wave patterns are seen.

Alfa : 7-14 cycles per minute.

Beta : 14-17 cycles per minute.

Delta : 3-7 cycles per minute.

Theta : 0-3 cycles per minute.

In short, we produce our stress at the beta level. Our tryst with the subconscious and spirituality is at the alpha level. The alpha level can be stimulated by meditation which is an experience in itself. You might need a guru to guide you through the right nuances.

What we have to accept is that we are created in the true likeness of GOD and we are divine. We can communicate with the universe and the sub conscious of others by telepathy. Only thing is that there is little or no awareness of our spirituality in the younger generation and as a fall out, neither is there any belief.

A few years ago, I was suffering from an acute bout of tennis elbow in my left arm. I was almost incapacitated. Just then, my good friend Anita Bansal, asked me to accompany her into a Reiki session. I went, very reluctantly, for I was a total non believer of such mumbo jumbo stuff. Here I was, a practioner of the age old accepted art of allopathy. But being open to every thing, I went along. It was a long drawn out session and at the end of the day, the lady Reiki master said, "Now that the energy has passed through your arms, any one having joint pains, frozen shoulder or tennis elbows must have been cured."

I thought, "Hey. I am the prime candidate for healing."

And I moved my elbow and presto! The tennis elbow was gone. Just like that. It has been been almost 7 years since that fateful day and I have never suffered from that malady again.

Since then, I have asked many a sufferer of tennis elbows to get attunement in the first degree Reiki as a part of the treatment of this ailment. It has been successful every time, just as it had cured me.

I became a very avid practitioner of Reiki and since I was a doctor, I had a ready supply of people on whom I could practice my new found skills. I got too cocky and at one point of time, if there was a patient with pain in the abdomen, I would not even take the history. I would just ask the person to lie down on the table and would put my hands on his abdominal area and his pain would disappear in about one to one and a half minutes. Till one day, a patient walked through the door and before I could ask her about her problem, she blurted, "Doctor, just put your hands on my tummy. My peptic ulcer is working up!" Needless to add that I did just that and her pain disappeared and so did she with a quick thank you, as if that is what I was meant to do.

The most mind boggling incident was when a friend walked into my clinic and said, "Doctor, my father-in-law is very sick and as we speak, he might already be dead. But we would like you to see him." I am sorry to say this, but I was very reluctant to go because I wanted them to take the patient to a hospital at that point of time. What would a private practitioner be able to do. More over, there were chances that the patient would already be dead.

But the daughter was so insistent that I had to go. As it turned out that the patient was a 90 year old doctor on oxygen and already producing the death rattle. In my practice of 32 years, I have rarely seen a man survive longer than 5 minutes after the death rattle. I was one confused man that day. The blood pressure and pulse were not recordable and his veins had collapsed and he was clearly in shock. I had nothing to do, so I thought I would try Reiki on him. I got the two sons-in-law to hold his hands in a special heart mudra. And, I put my hands on his heart.

I had never done this before, so I did not know what to expect.

I sat there, thinking that if this man dies, I might get beaten up. Because these good people had brought in a doctor who would perform some miracle and save their father and here I was dealing in mudras and sitting with my head bowed and hands on the chest.

One boy ventured, “Doctor, are you doing Reiki?”

I got a shock when after 15 minutes of whatever I was attempting, the death rattle disappeared! It just disappeared! I had never seen that happen. I now could feel the pulse! But I dare not move, so I stayed in my position for another 15 minutes. The two had to keep on with the heart mudra. After 15 minutes, I decided to see what the good old blood pressure was. Did I get another jolt? Yes! Man! I got one of about 1000 volts. His BP was 120/80 mm Hg!

Now when any non believer or a scientific person reads such things, he thinks "This is humbug! A figment of imagination!" Obviously, this is exactly what you all must be thinking. This guy is lying just to make us believe that we are divine and that we too have the power.

But this man survived long enough to reach the hospital after I took his ECG, which showed only some strain and the injection of lasix. He lived for 6 months. I was called to see him again for some other ailment and I heard, he died later because of natural causes. If this had not happened to me, I would never have believed it myself. But it did and I had a host of confused people who had been shocked into silence. So shocked was everyone, that the person who had called me paid me Rs 200 instead of the usual Rs 500 that I charged for a home visit. I think he felt that since I had done nothing, so I deserved just a token!

And then there was a golfing couple who were sitting in the Gazebo. The husband was holding on to his neck and I heard him say, "It really is hurting!" as I was passing by. Something made me stop and ask, "What happened?"

He said, "There are bees on the 11th green and one of them stung me on the neck." I asked him to show me the neck. He was right. The whole area was red and swollen. It must have been painful, so I said, "See, I haven't done this for bee stings before, but let me try."

So I put my hand on his neck and since we are always in a hurry to play on, I gave him Reiki for only one or two minutes maximum and when I removed my hands .....Lo! Wonder of wonders, the swelling and the redness had gone. The pain had gone and there was a small wheal where he had been stung. The poor guy looked up and asked me, "What did you do?"

What could I say? I said let's play some real golf now!

Are you with me so far?

Mind you, I am a qualified allopathic doctor with a post graduate degree. If I have to be convinced about some healing technique, I have to have proof. And boy! Did I get proof!

To cure chronic diseases like, diabetes, anxiety disorders etc it has to be a total body Reiki. It takes about an hour and in those days, I would do five cases a day. You would be surprised to know that one of them was given distance Reiki!

There has to be an end to everything some time. There was this gentleman, who had severe diabetes and was a bad case of anxiety. After the first week of total body Reiki, his blood sugar dropped to 68 mg from a level of 294 mg. I had to reduce his insulin in a hurry. He did very well after that and was put on oral drugs after 21 days. In those days, there was also a cardiac case I was doing. He too became better, but you see, shortly after that I turned out to be a diabetic from a person whose sugar had never gone beyond 110 mgs to 290 mgs and I had to undergo angioplasty. Now a lot of people will disagree that Reiki makes the healer suffer, but I know of people who have suffered and who have given it up as I have. The explanation is that all the pluses and minuses have to take place in this universe itself. If I take away someone's disease, someone else has to get it to keep things in proper equilibrium. So what easier place than the guy who is doing the Reiki in the first place?

The reason I wanted to tell you about Reiki, is that I want you to be aware of this world. There is so much which we don't know about, and it is not in the field of education. I am sure of at least one thing ....WE are divine. We have powers we don't know anything about.

For example the power of healing through prayer. In his book "Medicine, Prayers and Miracles" Dr. Bernie Seigel, a cancer surgeon tells of his personal cases, where such miraculous cures took place in his hospital just by the power of faith and prayer.

When I got scared of Reiky, I found myself falling head first into Silva method. The originator of this technique was Jose' Silva of South America. He was the first person to heal people with the Alfa level meditations. I was impressed by the first person story of a merchant navy officer, whose Captain had succeeded in locating an important piece of equipment, which had been lost in the sea after a storm which had raged for 7-8 days. No one could imagine where the waves would have taken it after the storm. But he used the alfa level and found it!

I found it difficult to follow till Dr.Vijay Laxmi of Chennai taught me her own easier version of the alfa meditation. Since then many miracles have taken place. My definition of a miracle is: "any happening for which you do not have an explanation," is a miracle. After alfa meditation, many things have happened. One could easily call them co incidences, but then too many of them began to happen. The most interesting one of them was the time when my wife could influence my mind to stop drinking alcohol for a record breaking period of 70 days! I can say that I had nothing to do with it and neither was I aware that she had any thing to do with my stopping! It was later that I got suspicious and asked her about her role. I also met a young girl of 12, who cured herself of a debilitating acne, which many a good doctor failed to cure. The best part of this technique is that I could reach the meditative state in a matter of minutes. Earlier techniques would take a long time and that too with great difficulty. I am happy to report that I am still meditating in the alfa.And so does my wife. If you are inclined, make sure that you have a Guru to initiate you correctly. You too could interact with the universe, with others through telepathy, you could heal yourself or improve your grades in school and college.

As far as the physical fitness goes, it is elementary. All that one must do, is to be physically active, eat and drink within limits. But if you look around, especially in the early morning hours, you would see these grossly obese people trying to undo what they have done i.e remove the layers of fat that they so successfully accumulated on their bodies. That is why I want you to carefully read this book and refrain from letting this happen to you. Even in your schools and colleges, you see the fattest children that one can imagine. These are the effects of becoming couch potatoes .... watching cable TV all the time while eating chips and burgers and sipping the dreadful colas.

So go out in the open, play games and burn the calories you have taken in. Imagine, even adding 3 gms every day, will result in a kilogram in a year. In 10 years, you have already gained 10 kilos! Hence, keep the calories in deficit.

But let me forewarn you that it is a very difficult task. If you have decided to have one measly pizza, you have already taken in 1764 calories. I am not counting the Pepsi that goes along with it. To burn these calories, you will be shocked to hear about the workouts in the gym, the swimming and the jogging that you will have to do.

By the way, you would burn roughly 11 calories per minute jogging and if you have stamina to jog for 30 minutes, you would burn up only 330 calories. But most people can't jog for 30 minutes! I can't, that is for sure.

Swimming would help you burn 16 calories per minute. If you can swim non stop for 30 minutes after your jog, you would burn an additional 480 calories. So now you have succeeded in burning 810 calories. Only 954 calories left to burn.

But then the pizza wasn't the only thing that you ate, did you? There was the yummy breakfast, juices, ice creams and the chicken tikkas. All that you have to do, is to calculate the calories and then put on your swimming trunks or your jogging shoes and run to Ambala and back. Hopingly, the calories might have evaporated by the time you reach back home.

Suppose you haven't burnt all these calories, they just get added up. 7700 calories makes 1 kgm of solid fat. In other words, if you have to reduce 1 kgm of fat, there has to be a calorie deficit of only 7700 calories!

The other side of the story, is taking in too few calories and literally starving on not only calories, but also nutrients and essential vitamins and minerals. There has to be a balance between the two aspects of food.

So what am I getting at? What a young growing adult requires daily is only 1800 to 2400 calories, according to Indian standards.

Hence, don't go beyond that mark. If possible, keep it below that and stay off from sugar. Keep your taste buds under control and remember we in India, are sitting on a time bomb of diabetes and heart disease. It is up to you to control.

There is one aspect of nutrition and supplemental therapies that I must talk about here, is the value of anti oxidants, Vitamin B complex especially, vitamin B12 and folic acid. They are hugely relevant to us, especially to the young ones. Vitamin B12, as we are finding out now, along with folic acid are very important in reducing a substance called Homocysteine. This substance has been incriminated in cerebro vascular strokes, heart attacks and osteoporosis. Folic acid also reduces the incidence of birth defects.

A few years back, if you had asked me the value of supplements, I would have told you that they are not required, but we know better now. We do require supplements in the form of multivitamins and proteins. Despite the fact that our young ones seem to be over fed and are grossly obese, their basic problem is under nutrition. Their diets lack the basic ingredients, which make food healthy.

It is no good to be studying so hard to be doctors, engineers, IT professionals and then going down with heart attacks, hypertension and diabetes at age 30! This was the basic idea behind writing this book.

Ladies and gentlemen, gifts are gifts only if they are looked after by the receipient. It is no use, if you throw the gift in the cellar or dump it in the waste paper basket. This gift from God is so unique that it should be kept on a pedestal and worshipped.

The best way to do that would be to look after yourselves and stay healthy. There are things like genetics against which we can't do much at this point of time. Scientists are busy finding ways and means to rectify genes too. But we should look after those aspects of our being that we can.

There is so much awareness in the general population about disease which was missing in our times. There is knowledge about the family history regarding diseases such as diabetes, heart disease and hypertension. And if, despite knowing so much, the youth of today still get swayed by advertisements about colas and the pizzas, disregarding their health, then it would be foolishness on their part.

Just remember, there is so much sugar in the colas and the bottle goes down beautifully in a matter of seconds. And no one thinks twice about having the second and third ones. Please, parents and you young readers, STOP INSULTING YOUR BODIES.

Just ask the people who endorse these products if they drink colas themselves? I am sure they don't.

I discussed this subject with a good friend, Mr H.P. Singh. He said, "You are the wrong man to write on this subject."

I asked, "Why?"

He said, "I shall tell you a very old story. It goes something like this:"

There was once a little boy who loved eating jaggery (gud), almost to a fault. His mother realised that she could not rectify this habit of his on her own. So she took him to a swamiji, and asked him to advise her son not to eat so much gud. Swamiji agreed to do so, but only after one week. He asked her to come back with the boy the next week.

The lady was back after a week. Swamiji looked at the boy and said, "Son, don't eat gud", the lady was surprised and said "Is that all? You could have told him this last week."

Swamiji said, "No! Last week I was eating gud myself, so how could I tell him not to eat it?"

So, Mr H.P. Singh said to me, "I know that you are a great fan of Ganesh and your paunch is also very similar to his. How can you give advice on health, if you can't look after yourself."

I agreed with him and started looking after myself. I joined a gymnasium and actively exercised for 2 hours every day. I look better. Any way, I haven't really reached the swami's level, but I am reaching there. Since I do practice the other aspects that I have talked about, therefore I sort of qualify to write this book for the younger generation, so that they do not commit the same mistakes as I did.

Like I have already said, in our times, there was paucity of knowledge. I was told to have ghee, butter and cream, since I was a national level badminton player and a body builder. They thought that these things were good for building stamina, and I loved gorging on them. So much so, that I went totally beserk. Can you imagine, even in the year 1974, my mother-in-law was told by my mother, that I love fresh malai (cream). So as a new son-in-law, I was made to eat a full bowl of fresh cream, laced with either jam or sugar every time I went to visit them.!!!!

I remember, I would look at my mother-in-law with awe and think, "Wow, this lady really loves me"

Imagine me, at age 24, a doctor, slurping a full bowl of cream!

Later, my protests would be drowned by the simple logic of a sage "Don't worry, nothing happens because of cream!!"

These small things and the subsequent alcohol did make things happen. I went from a healthy 61 kilograms to a 104 kilograms giant in just 4 years!!

The title of this book could easily have been :

"Understanding life ......at the right time!".

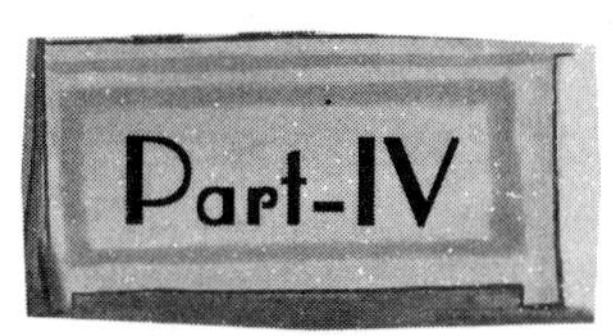
Part-IV

Attitude of Revolt in the Young and Upcoming

I have had a lot of pleasant responses from young boys and girls from all over the country after PLEASE, MOM! IT'S MY LIFE hit the stands. Analysis revealed that **these children were the ones who thought about life seriously and some had difficulties handling issues they faced in their day to day life.** As a consequence, I too began to look at teenagers and young adults more closely. As far as I am concerned, youngsters are the same everywhere, in the good old Punjab or Tamil Nadu. I concede that the ones in the North are more garrulous and louder than their counterparts in other states, but the issues are the same.

The more I delved into this issue, stranger seemed the facts. The first thing that came up was:

Why are children allergic to authority? Why is that the moment they come face to face with authority, some kind of a mini volcano starts simmering within them?

I too was young. Most of us looked up to our parents with awe. We acknowledged them as our parents who knew what was best for us. We kind of listened to them most of the time. In our time, late night parties were virtually non existent. After all, where could we go? The 6 to 9 pm show was all we had. There were no TVs and naturally no VCDs or DVDs. If we had to pass our time in a well meaning way, we had to go outdoors and play games. **You might find it funny, but I first came across a tape recorder when I was in the 10th class! I owned my first radio at the age of 13. The condition set by my father was a first division in matriculation, which I more than fulfilled.** Tantrums were of no avail. Those days, we had to listen to our parents, like it or not. Even teachers were hugely respected. After so many years, if I come across a teacher of mine, I still touch his or her feet. How many of today's children do that out of respect? Very few. Why? At least, in Punjab, they still do. I do not know about other places. I am sure those children whose parents taught them this simple thing must be respecting teachers the way my generation did.

In the last one year, ever since this book was released in April 2006, I have spoken to about 10, 000 children in schools in and out of Chandigarh. I have also spoken to about 400 odd parents about how they should bring up their children. A lot of these children felt that the young of today are about 20-30 years ahead of their parents. I smile and ask them a series of questions. I will ask you the same questions too.

How many of you stood up the moment you were born?

How many of you started walking the moment you were born?

How many of you started talking the moment you were born?

How many of you started eating and drinking on your own, the moment you were born?

How many of you started cleaning yourselves after you had passed stools or urine at birth?

If you answer **'yes'** to any of these questions, I will agree to the statement that your generation is definitely ahead, without a moment's hesitation. Mind you, animals start standing, walking and eating on their own almost immediately after birth. But not the young of humans. So, if your answer is **NO** to these questions, how are you more evolved than your parents? They also couldn't do these things 30 years ago, and you can't do them either?

Some children said that they are exposed to such superior technologies which their parents had not even heard of. So does that make you 30 years ahead? No! It is technology that has advanced. We are basically where we started from. The only thing is that you know how to press more buttons and switches and you can interpret modern technology. After all, it was your parents and society that exposed you to modern technology. In any case, had you been born 20 years earlier, you would not have been able to do some things that your parents did. After all, they were the pioneers of their times.

O.K., even if you *are* 30 years ahead of your parents, look around you. Do you like what you see? Do you see young ones talking on mobile phones while driving two wheelers and four wheelers, when the police has specifically banned it, young ones driving like maniacs through crowded areas, young girls drinking themselves silly at 3 pm in the afternoon, young boys and girls indulging in sexual antics in public places, at ages where their primary duty should be to study? Young ones getting into road rage and killing people, young ones drinking and driving. Never has the intake of drugs been so high in young people as today. Young ones committing suicide at a tender age of 10? Why is he killing himself when he doesn't even know what living is? What is this? Advancement by any chance!

I have been at the receiving end of some such advancements too. The other day while driving into Sector 17 market in Chandigarh, I got stuck in a jam. The person behind me began honking incessantly. I got out and told him that his honking will not clear the traffic ahead of me and in any case, I had no mood to sleep there that night. **There was a gentleman hardly 22 years of age at the**

wheel. He had some words for me which made me feel so ashamed and glad at the same time that he wasn't my son.

Another time, a lady parked her car in a bottleneck and went off to buy Diwali crackers from a shop. This led to a serious traffic jam. I asked the lady if that was the right place to park the car. Lo and behold! Out came the daughter and stood over me and shouted, "Is this the way to talk to my mother? You are so rude! Just for that, I will not move my car. What will you do now?"

I said: "I am senior to your mother by a decade and if she hasn't taught you how to talk to people of my age, then I can see where society is heading."

What I am trying to say is that advance and progress should be visible, palpable and positive. By drinking more and starting earlier, taking drugs, by being sexually promiscuous, by being out late at night, by being short tempered, by being selfish and self centered where we only think of what others can do for us and not what we can do for others (here, by others, I mean our parents, siblings,

society and the country), I see nothing positive coming from being advanced.

I would like the young to be well behaved and set an example for others to follow in evolution. Instead of aping the West, we should show the world what Indians of yesteryears had in terms of morality, behavior, and respect for elders, especially parents. Mind you, there is a whole new generation of Americans who do not subscribe to premarital sex, do not smoke and do not do drugs. They call themselves Christians. If you have to ape anyone, why not make these youngsters role models?

Only in India can a Shravan Kumar be born; a son born to blind parents who wanted him to take them on a pilgrimage. This son never made his parents feel that they were blind. He never questioned their intentions. They could have seen

only through his eyes. What good would it do for them? How could he carry them on his shoulders? He did not argue on any of these issues. He just carries them on his shoulders all around until he is killed by a king called Dashrath, who mistakes him for a deer.

In today's world, Shravan Kumar would have brought forth a fountain of logic as to why they would be better off sitting at home. He has to do some important work at the office which will bring him some pats on his back, and then again, it might not.

But I met a modern Shravan Kumar the other day. His name is Siddharth and he belongs to the state of Haryana. His mother wanted to go on a modern pilgrimage, to a naturopathy centre for two months. So he dumped all his work and took off to take his mother on that pilgrimage. He also told me that in his home, no one sat down in his mother's presence till asked to. When his father came back from work, all activity in the home ceased. The father, the master of the house, the bread winner of the family had arrived. Everyone was duty bound to make it clear to the father that he had come to his kingdom, where he was the master of all he surveyed. He did not work so hard for nothing. That the whole family was deeply indebted to him. That they acknowledged his deeds. What he said was a command. Even when Siddharth was to get married, the grandfather met Siddharth's future father-in law, who said that he had given birth to a daughter. She will not be put up in the market as a commodity. If he was interested to accept her as a daughter- in-law, on the strength of the family name and respect, do so, otherwise there will be other proposals. So impressed was the grandfather that he said 'yes' for the alliance, bought some sweets home and

announced to Siddharth's mother that he had said 'yes' to her future daughter-in-law. No one argued.

Mind you, Siddharth is not an illiterate goof. He belongs to your generation, having studied in a convent school and is a University topper in law. Incidentally, his wife turned out to be a Punjab University topper too and a looker at that.

How I wish I knew this family and learn from it.

I have a wish. One day, I will go to the state of Haryana to meet Siddharth's parents.

There is a long list of wishes I have. Foremost of them is the dream that all girls will once again become as modest as the women in our backward families were.

I would rather be ensconced in my 20 years backward cocoon. The endearing chunni was a sign of a woman's modesty then.

What has this forwardness given us? Agreed, you have to wear fewer clothes. But does this buy anyone any respect? I have a friend whose house gives me the shivers. No, there are no ghosts there. Only his daughters. **The clothes they wear embarrass me to no end. I can't keep looking at the floor all the time, can I? No, neither do I have a dirty mind.**

I go back to comparing again. In my time, if my wife had something on which was too obvious, she had to go back and change. These days something has happened to young husbands. They seem to have lost all their confidence. They are overdressed themselves but they love to flaunt their wives whose attire leaves nothing to imagination? Why are they doing this? I suppose to be one up on their friends. They seem to be making a statement here ......that my wife is more beautiful than yours, if you don't agree, you can see for yourselves.

I might belong to a backward era, but I would like someone to explain to me the concept of the beauty pageants. How do they enhance the respect of women? I am sick of hearing dialogues like the liberation and empowerment of women. Is this liberation? Pray how does flaunting empower them?

One thing that should be remembered is that no self-respecting family accepts girls as their daughters-in-law if they dress in their mini dresses for the 'dekho'. At that time, everyone expects the soon-to-be-bride in traditional clothes. Even the boy, who loves his girlfriends in that attire, would look down upon this one.

I have been a boy myself and I must tell you that **all boys have double standards. There is one set for the girl in the street and there is another for the one whom they will marry.**

Please, girls. Don't do this to yourselves. Respect yourselves and others will respect you. There is a saying in the vernacular:

"Apni izzat apney haat mein hoti hai."

Infatuation

I got another sweet letter from a girl saying that I had touched nearly all topics but conveniently left out a topic which was very important for teens.

A topic they can't discuss with too many people, least of all their parents. Friends will always mislead them, because of the limited knowledge that they themselves possess.

I guessed it right first time.

She wanted me to discuss INFATUATION.

The dictionary meaning is itself self explanatory. **Fatuus** means **foolish. Infatuate** means **affect person with extreme folly.**

But then we have these giggly teens who find the opposite sex very attractive. Even boys go through this phase. Later on, when they look at their past follies, this phase embarrasses them the most. Children are ready to run away from their homes. To them this seems the most important thing in their lives. The person who is sympathetic to their cause is their best friend and those who are not are their sworn enemies. The battle lines are very clear. That is the time when the parents, without their having any inkling of what is happening, become enemy *numero uno!*

To the people who are suffering from this malady, it is a very serious business. Since most of them are in schools and colleges, they neglect their studies. Sadly, academics are the major losers here. They will spend hours day dreaming, thinking about their so-called loved one. Most of the time, the other party is not aware of what this one is suffering. And then there are cases where the other party doesn't care a hoot! I have seen foolish young ones slash their arms with blades. They are careful not to slash the artery or they are not aware of the arterial effect. But you see this breed so many times with scars. People know immediately and make a mental note to stay away from them.

It isn't that only the young fall prey to this malady. I have seen grown ups acting like fools in exactly the same way as the young ones do. **But let me tell you that I am not too sure if there is a thing called love. I have also seen people falling head over heels in love, falling like a ton of bricks as they say, get married and then get divorced in less than a year! This is called a short story. The long stories belong to those whose relationships are nurtured by sacrificing couples, over a period of time during sickness and health and in happiness and sorrow.**

My advice to the young ones would be to stay away from these foolish notions of puppy love and bide their time. When their time comes, look with their brains rather than their hearts. Unlike Hindi movies where the movie ends when the two lovers get married, **real life begins after marriage. It is a commitment for life.**

Peer Pressure

I am grateful to the reader from Bangalore who pointed out that I had not touched upon an important subject that teens are routinely subjected to, namely 'Peer Pressure'.

I thought I already had, in the chapter on FRIENDS. When I went through it again, I found she was right, because I had not used the words 'Peer Pressure'. I had generalized the topic, using it to flay the drug habit and crime.

But I would still make a suggestion. Before reading this chapter, please go back and read the topic 'Friends' again.

The proverb '**birds of a feather flock together**' is important in this context. Also, the next line that says ***'Birds can't help it. But you as humans can sprout feathers of your own choice and choose the kind of people you want to spend time with!'*** is equally important.

Think about this and you will understand what I am trying to say here.

Peers are those people who are of your own age group with similar hobbies or in the same class.

It is said that people are affected by peer pressure. On the contrary, we succumb to it most willingly. The biggest reason is that we don't have enough self-confidence. We look up to other people, who we convince ourselves, are better, more intelligent, macho or richer than us. This pressure is not there just for teens; it is there for adults too, who succumb to it as easily as the teens. It could be related to our jobs, some familial feud or even political leaning.

Peer pressure is not all bad. There are peers who help us take decisions that we are finding very difficult to take on our own. We do it all the time due to lack of confidence in ourselves or in our own judgement. The good peers might keep you out of bad groups, get you to work harder in your studies, or join some sport that you would not have joined on your own. There are times when you want to do something but do not have the guts. Peer pressure might give you the necessary impetus.

If one has to do things or behave in a way which is alien to one's character only to join a peer group, then that is negative pressure. Here one might get involved in drugs, violence or bunking classes, lying to your parents or teachers. On your own, you might never want to do those things but just to be one of the gang or group, you act with bravado and do them.

I come from a family where no one ever imbibed alcohol. While studying in I.G. Medical College, Shimla, I met a person of royal lineage from Madhya Pradesh. He was in Shimla as a tourist and their group was short of cash. We invited them to stay with us so that they could extend their holidays. Let's call my royal friend Mr. Raghu. He stayed with me in my room in the hostel. After about two hours of our meeting, I was immensely impressed with whatever he did or said. I thought that pearls of wisdom dropped out of his mouth, the moment he opened it. In real life, he was routinely dishing out judgements to people of his kingdom, whatever that was. This was in addition to the fact that he was an engineering student. He was such a happy man and he drank everything that came under the purview of 'alcohol'. He insisted that I too take beer with him because that was the only thing we could afford at that point of time.

I refused because of the fact that I had never had it before. Moreover, I detested things which were bitter.

He suggested, "So what if no one in your family has had it before? As for the bitter taste, just dilute the beer with coca-cola."

I agreed just to please him. The concoction certainly pleased me. By the time he left Shimla, I had started on 'neat' beer. A few days later, I took my first shot of whisky, all this so that I would not be left behind the 'Royal' gentleman from Indore. He later on went on to become the Chief Minister of the state. That was peer pressure.

Normally, I would not lift my hand against anyone willingly. But then I joined my 'friends' in fights I would never have joined, had I listened to myself. Luckily I was never injured. If I had more confidence in myself, I would have clearly told the others to fight their own battles. But I would have been branded a coward, wouldn't I? No one likes that. Neither did I! So I joined them. I not only joined them, but was in the forefront just to prove a point. Wasn't it foolish? It definitely was, if I may say so myself. That is why I advise you to stay away from 'Negative Peer Pressure'.

Recently, we heard of two incidents which occurred in Delhi. They were passed off as road rage. In the first, five boys on two motorcycles were involved in a minor accident with a car. They got so agitated that they beat up the car driver and then one of them smashed a pot on the car driver's head which killed him instantly. Here was an open and shut case of peer pressure. One was the leader and the rest of them were sufferers of peer pressure. Just one of them was needed to restrain the others and the poor fellow would still be alive.

In the other incident, an advocate from Chandigarh was accosted on a flyover in Delhi. The idea was to rob him. But since there was some resistance from the advocate, they decided to teach him a lesson. One of them, who must have been the leader, suggested that they throw him off the flyover. They dragged him towards the railing with all intentions to give him flying lessons. The leader of the gang had convinced the other three about the feasibility of their intention. If the other three had used their brains, they would easily have decided that robbing someone in public was not such an intelligent idea, and throwing an innocent man down the flyover was totally an unnecessary and foolish act. The advocate used his presence of mind and saved himself, but that is a separate matter. This again was negative or bad peer pressure.

There are times when your peers might indicate subtly that you have to dress and behave in a particular way in order to be a part of the group. Despite your brain screaming away that it would not be very happy to comply, you still do what your peer group suggests. Obviously, something wrong is bound to happen. The peer group is not responsible. You are. You made the final decision, didn't you?

This reminds me of a story I heard on the FM radio. This particular RJ is like me. She has a collection of some beautiful stories. I never get a chance to listen to her full programme, so I don't know her name.

Anyway, the story is as follows:

Two teenage brothers go to their dad for permission to see a particular movie. They said their friends had praised the movie to heaven and back... a movie with a moral, the hero full of courage and patriotism... blah, blah and blah.

Luckily, the father had seen its reviews in the papers. It had nudity and a lot of immorality. So the father said that the movie was for children above 18 years of age and that too under parental guidance. Under the circumstances, he

was refusing permission because of the nudity and immorality it contained.

"But Dad!" said the two, "It has a moral; it tells us about courage and patriotism. It is a two hour movie and the scenes you talk about are hardly a few minutes!"

The father was firm in his decision and he persisted with a NO!

The boys went to their room and sulked, till a fine aroma of brownies being baked in the kitchen reached their olfactory cells.

"Dad is trying to be nice to us by baking brownies. I think he will let us go to see the movie after all!" one of them said hopefully.

By and by, the father brought them a plate of brownies. He told them that he loved the two of them very much. He had baked brownies for them especially with the best ingredients available. Organic stuff and all that! The boys were impatiently waiting for their father to finish the story so that they could eat them and then go for the movie. After all, their dad was feeling guilty for refusing permission for the movie and now he was trying to make up. But the father carried on and on.

"I have changed the recipe a little and added another organic material into them. But the amount is minuscule."

The boys asked what the last organic addition was. The father avoided telling them, but finally acceded.

"It is organic. I added a tiny amount of dog poop! I am sure the brownies will still have a wonderful taste. Try them."

The boys dropped their plates and announced that they would have none of the brownies.

"But I only put a small amount of dog poop. Overall, the brownies are great. Eat them and see for yourselves."

But the boys were adamant and looked at their fingers in disgust.

Then the father said, "Look at you. You refuse to eat these lovely brownies just because of a little amount of dog poop. But just because your friends told you that it is a great a movie despite the nudity and the immorality, you were ready to destroy your moral fabric and wanted to see the movie. Your morality is much more important than a little dog poop filled brownie, isn't it?"

The young boys came and hugged their father and apologized for being so naïve.

This is another aspect of negative peer pressure.

Since peer pressure is a part and parcel of our lives, what do we do? Simple! Follow the steps given below:

- Have lots of confidence in yourself.
- Choose the right kind of friends.
- Be very certain in your mind what you would do and what you won't. Then no matter how much pressure anyone puts on you, it won't matter, for you would have the confidence in yourself and your actions.
- This brings us to the point of the good and the bad things. Smoking, drugs, shop lifting, lying to your parents, group violence are the bad ones. Studying well, working hard

in your chosen field, good moral behaviour are the good ones.

- Many times, your parents have to shoulder the brunt of the peer pressure that you are suffering in school. There are rich children in your class who have expensive laptops, designer shoes, watches and clothes. You MUST have them too. Our parents might not be in a situation where they can accede to your whims and fancies. If you are not clever enough or understanding enough, this small thing can trigger an intra-familial war! Please, don't make your parents lose their self-respect.
- Experimenting with sex is your decision which you take on your own after going into the pros and cons of it. You don't have to do it just because everyone else is doing it. Even having a boyfriend is not necessary. If you feel the overpowering need and after making sure that the friend is indeed of good moral values, do it. But all these decisions have to be yours and are not to be taken under peer pressure.
- Once you have the required self-confidence, you can be a leader and exert positive influence on your peers. It doesn't have to be the other way round.
- If the pressure of behaving or dressing in a particular manner is necessary to get into a group and if you don't like to do that, then it would be better to decide against joining the group than to let yourself be led.

These things are easier said than done. You can produce n number of excuses to wriggle out of the situation if you don't want to use the good old 'NO' emphatically. You can blame some of your physical malady or your sports training or even blame it on your parents (my mom would kill me or she would die if she saw me smoking or taking drugs or having sex).

Finally, I would say that you have to take responsibility for your decisions, whatever they may be.

Best of luck for that! Believe me… you will need it.

Summarizing

There are a few important things that we take home from here.

The first and foremost thing is that this book needs to be read repeatedly. There is no way that you can soak it up in one reading and say you have got it all. I have had to read it at least 40 times and then too, it requires revision. We are made that way. We tend to overlook things. There will be times when you forget to be anger-free or you tend to revert to your attitude of revenge, instead of forgiving the person who has harmed you. It happens to me all the time and when I re-read the book, I catch myself saying, "Ah-haan, you forgot this!"

Remember what Mother Teresa said in the beginning of this book? See, Didn't I tell you? We tend to forget. So, please go back and read it again.

This book is all about busting the omnipresent stress because of which we become diseased (dis-ease). If you can master stress, at any age, you won't suffer so much. Though , "younger the better is the rule". It is not that you can really master something like stress. You have to rise above the issues that cause it and not let it affect you to harmful levels.

Remember, stress is not all bad. We need it to push us, so that we can perform better in life.

This book is all about discovering what works for you. But there are some basic things that you cannot overlook. There is no way that we can deny or forget the existence of God. We have to be in a perpetual mode of thanksgiving, not just in the morning and at night. We have so much to thank him for, beginning with the life that he has given us, our parents, siblings, our country, the society we live in, and our friends.

We are divine. One doesn't know what God looks like. So one can't say that we have been created in his image. But one thing is sure. We are here not just to go through school, college, to get a job, earn tons of money and say that we have arrived. We are here to do greater deeds and not get sucked up in the quagmire of petty daily existence. Even for a person earning millions and doing nothing else, it is just a matter of figures and zeros. But before everything else, we have be good human beings. Everything comes after that.

Respect. This is one aspect that we have to accept. We just have to respect the hierarchy which means that we have to respect the authority of parents, siblings and teachers and then juniors have to respect seniors and vice versa. There has to be respect for each other at home, in school and in marriage. I have known two people, Khurshid and Sharif for the last twenty five odd years. They are the ones who have been doing the painting in my house every Diwali. They continue to do so. This year, I looked at them and realized that they too had grayed, and wondered how two people can work together for so long and never fight. The answer was self evident. Khurshid, the talkative type, is the boss. Sharif is the sober one, almost effeminate. Sharif has accepted the fact that Khurshid is the boss and never contests his authority. He only suggests. So where is the nidus for conflict? Tell me, how many of us can really do that. Our egos will come in the way. This aspect of our lives is sorely missing. Hence we see so many conflicts in every sphere of life. There is, however a difference between sycophancy and respect. If you look around, you will see sycophants overflowing every scenario. These people have no respect for anyone.

I don't know what you all will end up doing. But make choices and then take responsibility for them. There is no sense in the blame game. No matter what hand is dealt to us by God, we have to accept it and then take a decision to improve upon it. If we just sit back and lament our luck, then we will most certainly end up getting stressed ourselves, and jealous of those who are supposedly in a better situation than us. Many times, the grass seems to be greener in the other man's yard. It might not actually be that. And then we appoint ourselves judges of all and sundry and pass reckless judgment on the ones who have made it or are in the process of doing that. This is a huge reason for being stressful.

I agree that this world is no longer a perfect place for us to live in. It is all our doing. We should remember that we are the ones who have made it imperfect by our ever increasing demands. Materialistic and otherwise, they keep on increasing. We have lofty standards of how our parents should be, how our homes should be, how our husbands and wives should be, how our children should be, what designer stuff we should be owning. And if all these things are not up to our standards, then heaven help our stress levels. The anger comes in cascading, ready to drown everything that comes in it's way. Pray tell me, how many times have we done any self introspection? Only to see where do we stand, and how far do we come up in the scale of our own standards? Do that, please, once in a while.

Happiness is our birthright. To give happiness and to accept happiness from whoever wants to give. That brings us to the point of giving and taking. Give till it hurts and accept what is given with grace. For there will be no givers if there are no receivers. It is said that "you can never make a man happy who is not at peace with himself, and you can never be at peace with yourself if you want every one to be happy with you!"

Finally, what takes us down is our ego and it is always false. There is no true ego. Ego is the facial mask of who we are in society, and is fear based. The fear is always of losing what we have. Thus we are always scared of shadows which chase us.

Never be scared of shadows. Shadows only mean that there is a bright light shining somewhere nearby! I believe that the bright light is GOD! He has his plans for us. We will receive his Grace when the right time arrives!

So, my dear friends! Why the hurry!!?

Be happy!

Few opinions about the book

An outstanding and an interesting book with vivid illustrations. Reading it will make both parents and children wiser.

—J.P. Singh
Principal
St. Kabir Public School, Chandigarh

"Please, Mom! It's My Life" is a book not only for teenagers, but also for parents, grandparents, teachers, counsellors, psychologists and medical practitioners, who are concerned about the well-being of their wards.
This book is unique in the sense that it highlights issues connected with life-styles, attitudes and values of our society, and provides insight to the mind of the young adolescent.

—Dr.(Mrs.) Shayama Chona, Padma Shri
Principal
D.P.S. R.K. Puram, Delhi

*In this day and age, when there seems to be a growing alienation between us and our children, primarily on account of the mind-boggling rate of change, a book such as **"Please, Mom! It's My Life," becomes almost like a lifeline**. We all need help, and this book gives it!*

—Dev Lahiri
Principal
Welham Boys' School, Dehradun

*Dr. Jaideep Chadha's book, **"Please, Mom! It's My Life"** touches upon every aspect of adolescent world with impeccable understanding. The stories that have been incorporated in the book have simple, yet powerful message of refreshing optimism.*
This is a book for everyone who wants to be empowered.

—Sister Reenet
Principal
Little Flower Convent School, Panchkula

Once you start it—you can't put it down!

A witty and humorous insight into the adolescent mind. The author being a 'Saint-healer' is able to guide the young mind gently and without preaching. A must read for all youngsters to channelise their energies in the right direction. The advice is through stories and personal anecdotes. The language is simple and very readable and is sure to build a strong and happy citizen and prevent the new generation from going astray.

—C.P. Bansal IPS,
Director General of Police & MD, Panchkula

To attain a certain level of maturity at a young age, this is a "must-read" book, which gives a clear-cut view of the attitude which one should possess in life.

—Nikki Latta
Age–15 years

I would advise that this book be made available to one and all in this society. To help the society to get stress free. Stress free society is a healthy society. I would like to congratulate and appreciate the work of Dr. Chadha and I would also like to request him to keep writing such inspirational and useful books for the society.

—Neelam Khosla
Red Cross Society
Patiala District

*It was indeed a pleasure to read your book, **"Please, Mom! It's My Life."** It gives tremendous insight about healthy interaction with children.*

—Mrs Neeta Jauhar
Director
Springfields Public School,
Yamuna Nagar, Haryana

*My life is already changing because of **"Please, Mom! It's My Life"**—a great book.*

—Nikkhar Budhiraj, Delhi
Age–18 years
(Engineering student)

The Funny Side of GOLF

"After PG Wodehouse's gold stories, this book was among the most thoroughly enjoyable volumes. I have ever come across."

—V.N. Narayanan
Editor-in-chief, The Tribune

"An entertaining booklet."

—Khushwant Singh
Acclaimed author

And I thought Golf was an abbreviation for—

G : GERIATRIC

O : ORGANISATION OF

L : LAME &

F : FEEBLE

Pages: 176
Price: Rs. 100/- • Postage: Rs. 15/-

Marriage Rocks!

A Prescription for a Happy Wedded Life

Marriage Rocks! A Prescription for a Happy Wedded Life is an antiodote for all those who consider marriage to be a 'poison'. Marriage is actually a double-edged sword—everyone dreads the pains and nuisances associated with it, at the same time being more than willing to be slain. This book aims at obliterating all such stereotypes bracketed together with this institution. The idea is, basically, to intimate the readers with the duties and responsibilities that one needs to fulfil while going through the married life and also the steps that could be taken to make this journey a smooth sail. In the ndian scenario, a myriad of relationships come as a package deal with wedding, dealing with which often fades its beauty. This book would ensure that your wedded life comes out of its sombreness, and you emerge victorious like a phoenix, proudly saying, 'Marriage Rocks!'

Pages: 180
Price: Rs. 120/- • Postage: Rs. 15/-

By the Same Author

Vinculum

Vinculum in essence means a stepping stone, an isthmus, and that is what this book is. It is an isthmus between adolescence and maturity, between dreams and reality and between happiness and sorrow.

Vinculum is a simple, heart-warming tale of five adolescents from different backgrounds thrown together in an environment as fascinating as a medical college, in a locale as romantic as Shimla.

Excerpts from various newspapers

Vinculum, a rather unusual synonym that stands for "stepping stone", the title of his first published novel takes Dr. Jaideep Chadha, a city-based cardiologist and consultant psychiatrist into the league of successful writers. — ***Times of Chandigarh***

...the book is an isthmus between adolescence and maturity and between happiness and sorrow, and also captures the locales of Shimla. — ***The Indian Express***

Vinculum [is a] heart-warming novel about five adolescents from different backgrounds growing up in a medical college. With Shimla as the backdrop, the novel becomes all the more romantic and enchanting. — ***Hindustan Times***

Demy Size • Pages: 178
Price: Rs. 95/- • Postage: Rs. 15/-